Soulful & Successful Business

SOULFUL AND SUCCESSFUL BUSINESS

First published in 2021 by Dragonfly Publications.

Copyright © Nicole Bayliss, 2021

All rights reserved. The moral rights of the author have been asserted under *Copyright Amendment (Moral Rights) Act 2000*.

Except as permitted under the Australian *Copyright Act 1968* (for example, a fair dealing for the purposes of study, research, criticism or review), no part of this book may be reproduced, stored in a retrieval system, communicated or transmitted in any form or by any means without prior written permission.

ISBN: 978-0-9875138-6-1

Printed by Lightning Source.
Cover Design and Layout: Ben Crompton Design

For information on ordering further copies of the book or to contact the author please visit nicolebayliss.com.au

10 9 8 7 6 5 4 3 2 1

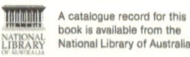
A catalogue record for this book is available from the National Library of Australia

Soulful & Successful Business

Spiritual Guidance for Succeeding in Your Own Business

Nicole Bayliss

Praise for Soulful & Successful Business

"Nicole Bayliss takes you deep inside yourself in this gem of a book! Imposter syndrome, comparison, fears, insecurities, money hangups! There are solutions du' jour for all. I adore this treasure!"

Cat Dillon, Registered Holistic Nutritionist/Proprietor Cat Dillon, RHN

"I love the message in this book! It redefines what success is without excluding the abundance we can have by doing what we love."

Valeria Teles , Healing Coach, Author and Host of A Quest for Well-Being Podcast

"This is a great read and is the perfect antidote if you are struggling with the ups and downs of being self-employed."

Sophie Ramsay, Founder and Owner of Flow Accounting, CPA

Foreward

Hello! I'm so glad this book has found you. So you're thinking of starting your own business, or perhaps you already have. You may even be a few weeks, months or years into it. **Did you know that on average one in three small businesses fail in their first year?** I do not want that for you. The Universe does not want that for you!

This book is here to help you grow a successful business and to enjoy every minute of it. My aim is to teach you some interesting spiritual concepts that will transform you and the way you perceive your business and your life. I will be sharing with you some key Universal Laws that must be abided by if you wish to travel the path of true success.

When you start the journey of working for yourself, it can be exhilarating and terrifying all at once. I know because I've been there. I had a lot of old ideas and beliefs to let go of, if I was to be true to myself and follow my deep desire to work for myself on my own terms. I want to share with you all that I have learned while travelling two parallel paths - the spiritual path and the path to creating a successful business.

In our modern world, spirituality and business have been

perceived as two very separate things; they may even be seen as opposing each other. This isn't true! We are here to live our best lives, and a part of that will be work, purpose and money. When we embrace the spiritual and bring it into the practical, miracles happen. We are all spiritual beings having a human experience, and we are here to bring our spiritual soul self into every aspect of our lives.

The world is changing. Many people are becoming disenchanted with working for large organisations and the old paradigm Age of Productivity "work ethic" is leaving them tired, stressed and unfulfilled. Many of us are wanting "something more" - more meaning, more day-to-day fulfilment and more love for our work.

I predict that the world will change through individuals emancipating themselves from the modern "global slavery system" whereby we feel trapped by work and financial circumstances. It's already happening everywhere; small businesses and organic networks popping up like daisies, and you can be a part of that wonderful change in this Age of Creativity.

In this book I will be sharing with you metaphysical truths and Universal laws, as well as stories and anecdotes that help illustrate an idea or a concept - some are from my own story and some are my clients' stories on their journey to success.

I'll also be giving you a Spiritual Business Plan, by providing journaling exercises, affirmations and prayers at the end of each chapter. You can download a free Spiritual Business Plan journal from my website nicolebayliss.com.au to accompany this book.

Be prepared that this book will change you at a foundational level - your beliefs, your understanding of how the Universe works and your relationship with the world "out there". It will release old paradigm thinking and conditioning that has prevented you from knowing how powerful you are and how successful, fulfilled and abundant you can be.

So if you are ready to expand your mind and your business, let us take this journey together. I'll be right there beside you every step of the way!

Love and Light,

Contents

True Success	13
The Power of Commitment	27
The Magic of Getting There	45
Transform Your Relationship with Yourself	61
Transform Your Relationship with Money	85
Transform Your Relationship with Life	107
Soulfully Successful Marketing	127
Your Ideal Work Day	153
Conclusion	173
About the Author	187

Chapter 1
True Success

True success has its roots in doing what you love and being happy and abundant because of it.

What does success mean to you? And, come to think of it, what exactly is success? In the Oxford dictionary, we are told that success is *"achieving something you want, have been trying to do or to get."* So the word "success" simply means to achieve something you desire. In our modern world however, we have overlaid onto the word "success" many ideas that are based on egoic values. The ego mind is the part of you that believes he or she is not enough, so in order to be enough, we must keep adding to ourselves.

The ego will have you believe that success will include, to some degree:

- Fortune
- Fame
- Power
- Status.

From my own personal experience, I have learned that these desires, if or when achieved, can prove to be empty victories if we don't also include values such as:

- Meaning and purpose
- Daily enjoyment
- Work/life balance
- Making a positive contribution or difference.

So what does success mean to you? What would it look like? A few years into being in my own business, I kept a journal and in it I wrote about the success I wanted to achieve.

- To help people using my gifts and talents
- To enjoy my everyday experience
- To make a good income (so as to do the things I love to do and have the things I'd like to own)
- To enjoy a balance between work and personal time
- To enjoy loving relationships
- To be healthy, fit and well.

It had taken a little while for me to work this out. Only a few years beforehand I had created a vision board that was clear evidence of an ego wanting to prove itself to the world. I was disappointed when my aims of making $1 million in my first year of business, flying first class around the world and writing a bestseller didn't eventuate! Alas, I learned that the Universe doesn't always give us what we want, but it does give us what we need.

So what happened to me in the two years between the "ego mind vision board" and the "true success journaling"? While nothing in particular happened on the outside (including not much business and not much profit!), quite a lot was going on on the inside. Disappointment and failure can be a wonderful opportunity to reassess, to reflect and to grow. That's what it did for me. Through experiencing the "failure" of my ego desires, I surrendered, and from this humble place, I experienced a deepening and an understanding of myself and the Universe. This was my soul awakening. I began to meditate more regularly and to pray. I had some wonderful conversations with the Universe and eventually the Universe and I came to an understanding. I understood what I was here to do and I also became aware that the Universe would support me totally when I dropped my ego and got on with it.

True success lies in doing what you love to do, making a positive difference in some way and being fulfilled and abundant because of it.

I call this "true success" - doing something that you know you are here to do and being provided for perfectly, so that you can go on doing it. So if you want to find fulfilment in your professional life, it is wise to think holistically. If the idea of true success appeals to you, ensure that your vision of success includes:

- Purpose
- Wellbeing
- Relaxation

- Relationships
- Financial goals
- Day-to-day happiness.

Caroline's story of ego success

Caroline came along to one of my early workshops Create the Life You Want, which was based on **The Universal Law of Attraction**, which deems that the more you visualise and feel that you have something, the more you draw it to you. We began with each person in the group introducing themselves and saying why they chose to attend the workshop. When it came to Caroline's turn, she couldn't speak. Instead, she burst into tears.

"I've achieved everything I thought I ever wanted. I have a successful business, a husband who loves me and three beautiful children, and yet I'm not happy. I feel stressed every day and I also feel that something's missing and I can't quite put my finger on what it is."

As the day progressed, what became apparent was that Caroline had manifested everything she thought she ever wanted, but not what her soul wanted for her. On a personal level, I could relate. Up until the age of 45, I too had manifested everything I thought I had ever wanted - a life that looked successful and abundant on the outside - but deep within I had felt an emptiness that I couldn't put into words.

We all have the ability to manifest - but manifest what? It was only after I experienced a chaotic midlife crisis that I finally surrendered to the Universe. I asked for the Universe to show me the way, and the Universe delivered, showing me my True Path and the way to True Success.

The Universal Law of Surrender

When our ego is in charge of our desires, it may manifest a life that is "successful" - that is, we achieve what we think we want, only to find out later that it wouldn't fulfill us. When we manifest from the True Self, we create all that will truly make us happy and abundant on every level. Manifesting True Success involves surrendering yourself and your purpose to the Universe. The Universe is the Divine Intelligence which knows what your True Path is. By surrendering, we are asking The Boss to take over and do for us what we cannot do!

Mike's story of a life out of balance

Mike had been very successful in business, but his personal life was a mess. His first marriage failed after ten years because he put all his time and energy into his business, and had very little left over for his wife and family. In his grief, Mike was drinking too much and was in emotional turmoil.

The Universal Law of Balance

When it all comes down to it, balance is the key to true success. **The Universal Law of Balance** deems that everything thrives when there is balance. We as human beings thrive when our lives are balanced. Truly successful people aim for balance in all areas of life. When we manifest out of balance, at least one area of our life will suffer. This is why I have written this chapter first - so as to start as we mean to go on. Without the right foundations, whatever is built won't be strong enough to last.

Love Your Business

If we want to get the foundations right and enjoy true success, we need to feel inspired about the work we do. We need to feel excited about the product we are selling or the service we are offering, and believe in that product or service, and that it can make a positive difference in the world. Whether you're an online business owner, a builder, a dog groomer, a beautician, a marketer, an accountant or a baker, believing that what you do is valuable is essential.

If you don't love and value what you do or what you sell, your business will not thrive for very long. Why? Because you are your business! When you feel love for what you do, you are constantly injecting your business with positive energy. Love is what creates abundance! And by abundance, I mean everything - money, clients, opportunities, happiness - everything! A lack of love for what you do will de-energise your business.

Does your business inspire you? Do you feel passionate about the service you offer or the products you provide? Feelings such as love, passion, inspiration and joy are the fuel for a successful business. These feelings create a vibration that will draw to you the clients, the business, the money, the opportunities and everything that you require to keep going and to thrive. The feelings that come with a sense of purpose are powerful.

The Universal Law of Dharma

The Universal Law of Dharma deems that each and every one of us is here for a reason. We all have strengths, talents and abilities and when we do what we love using these strengths, talents and abilities, we will create abundance as well as personal fulfilment. And not only this. Very often we discover that we have hidden gifts that we weren't even aware of when we chose to follow our hearts.

Most of us were not brought up with this message. We've grown up with the idea that in order to live in this world, we've got to "work", and the definition of "work" is doing something that you have to do so as to make a living, not something that you want to do so as to live your best life.

Those who dare to dream beyond working to survive are often labelled "dreamers" by those who are still stuck in this old way of thinking.

The Message My Parents Gave Me

As a child, I was a talented artist and every teacher I had encouraged me to do something with this talent in the future. However, while I acknowledge that my parents loved me and always wanted what they thought was best for me, I grew up being told that you had to *"work hard for a living"*, doing what you needed to do and not what you wanted to do. This wasn't my parents' fault. They had grown up in the war years and through the Great Depression.

When I wanted to attend the College of Arts after high school, I was told not to dream and to *"get a real job."* This belief that in order to survive, I had to do something that wasn't what I really wanted to do got hard-wired into me. Many years later, after doing many "real jobs", I took myself to art school. This was the start of me finding myself and my purpose.

Mission and Not Ambition

When we think about what we do in terms of purpose, instead of just a business and we do our work with love, we enter the Universal Flow. Most of us have been conditioned to focus on making money, and there are still so many messages out there today that are all about just the money, but if you make money your primary goal, you may manifest this desire but at the cost of being truly fulfilled.

Make your purpose - your business's mission - your goal. When you give it your passion, the money will eventually come, because passion creates. Passion is the Universal force coming through you as divine inspiration. Please don't think that I am saying that money is unimportant; because it is - and I've devoted a whole chapter to the topic of money in this book - but if you are focussing on the money alone, you're focussing on "getting". When you're focussing on "doing" because you really want to do it, you're focussing on "giving", and everything you give away returns to you.

The Universal Law of Giving and Receiving

The Universe works on exchange. We are here to both give and receive. Whatever we give away will come back to us, sometimes multiplied. If you spend or invest your money on something that is in your highest good and the highest good of all, you can be sure that the money will be returned to you multiplied eventually. If we are wanting to receive certain things, we must learn to give them first. This is **The Universal Law of Giving and Receiving**.

If we are thinking in terms of our purpose and our mission, we are thinking in terms of giving. From this place, we will create an energy vibration that is totally different to the vibration created by the old paradigm "work ethic". When you identify what the mission of your business is, you create a powerful foundational anchor to which all you need will be attracted. Your mission statement becomes the North Star of your business.

Realising my mission

In the early days of my business, I started out as a counsellor and reiki practitioner. I was meeting with clients from all walks of life, all experiencing different challenges and wanting to achieve different things. So what was my mission? I realised that no matter what the story or the desire of the client, I was here to assist with their transformation. And my own transformation was what was helping them the most - as I woke up and transformed my own mind, I was genuinely able to help others do the same. In my journal I wrote my mission statement:

"To assist others on their journey of transformation as I continue to transform myself."

A mission statement doesn't have to be long or complicated - just clear and to the point.

The Universe Wants You to Be Successful

The Universe wants for you what you want. The Universe wants you to be successful. It is not your enemy! Your only enemy is your ego mind that believes in lack and limitation or tricks you with ideas of grandiosity.

We have all been conditioned to believe in lack, hardship and struggle. Our DNA still contains the beliefs and traumas of our ancestors, many of whom only just got by and lived in survival mode. Our ego mind feeds us thoughts of fear, struggle, uncertainty and lack. So it's not your fault if you've not found success yet. There's some old programming that needs to be deleted and rewritten, and I will be doing just that with you throughout this book.

Whether you like it or not, your ego mind is taking this journey with you; you cannot kill the ego mind because it's a part of you. Becoming aware of the ego mind and acknowledging its fearful thoughts is how you transcend the ego mind. The Universe doesn't want your life to be hard! It wants you to live your purpose and enjoy every aspect of your life - in love, in purpose, in prosperity and in wellness.

For now, breathe, relax and surrender. Your success already exists, and it lies in doing something that you feel passionate about. You came here to live your purpose, to do what you love, to feel fulfilled, to make a positive difference and to create abundance.

When I chased after money, I never had enough.
When I got my life on purpose and focused on giving of myself
And everything that arrived into my life,
Then I was prosperous.

Wayne W. Dyer

Crafting Your Spiritual Business Plan

Exercise 1 - True Success

Take some time to contemplate and journal by answering the following questions. Write as much or as little as you wish.

What would I like to achieve in these areas of my life?

- Purpose
- Wellbeing
- Relaxation
- Relationships
- Financial goals
- Day-to-day happiness

What does true success mean to me?

What would my ideal working day look like?

Now take five minutes to visualise yourself enjoying this True Success until you are in the feeling place of it.

Exercise 2 - Your Mission

What is my mission?

I want you to close your eyes and take a few minutes now to ask yourself these questions and journal the answers.

- What am I giving?
- In what way am I making a difference?
- How does it make me feel?
- What is my mission?

Write your business mission statement.

Exercise 3 - A Prayer of Surrender

Be still and allow yourself to feel quiet and calm. Say the following prayer to the Universe:

I surrender to You who I am.
I surrender to You my desire to work on my own terms
And to find True Success and fulfilment.
I surrender to You my talents, skills and abilities.
Please show me the way.

Chapter 2
The Power of Commitment

Commitment creates a joint venture between you and the Universe

What does commitment mean to you? In the Oxford dictionary we are told that commitment is *"the state or quality of being dedicated to a cause, activity, etc."* To me, commitment means making a decision and sticking to it, and not giving up when the going gets tough. By committing, we put all of our energy fully into the choice we have made, creating a powerful vortex of energy. When we commit, the Divine moves with us and supports us. When we are non-committal, our energy is scattered and it is difficult to get traction and move forward. Commitment is the necessary foundation from which your business will grow.

My Story of Commitment

For a few years after I had received my qualification as a counsellor, I dithered. *"I might start my own practice some time in the future,"* I'd tell friends, not really believing my own words. It was easier to work for someone else, rather than start something from scratch and face the overwhelming self doubt and fear that loomed just beneath the surface. My hesitancy continued until I couldn't stand it anymore.

I'd taken a job as an executive assistant in an organisation in the city after my divorce, but I wasn't fulfilled. As I struggled with discontent, my circumstances got worse. The head of administration began micromanaging me, and refusing to give me the flexible hours the firm had promised me in my initial interview. In my personal life, I had set myself free from people who wanted to control and limit me, and yet here I was in an office job with a woman doing just that! When I was told that I wouldn't get the promised flexible hours over the summer holidays to spend with my kids, something in me snapped. I wrote my resignation letter that day.

"I don't ever want to work for someone else again," I decided. *"I want to be in charge of my life."* And with that, the decision to work for myself became clear. I had found my *"Why."*

A few weeks later I attended a one-day seminar on how to set up a counselling practice. It wasn't what I expected, but it was certainly what I needed.

"Are you going to be a Gonna Wanna Shoulda? Or are you going to do it?" shouted the speaker. I was shocked to hear that only a tiny percentage of people actually go into practice after qualifying as a counsellor, and the reason for this was that they didn't believe that they could succeed. Was I going to be one of those? Or was I going to take the plunge and become the counsellor I wanted to be?

"You gotta fake it till you make it," declared the speaker. By the end of the day, I was resolved to start my own business. I had loved studying and practising counselling but I still had a lot of self-doubt as to whether I could do it professionally and earn a living from it.

I took action anyway. I began by making a financial plan. I worked out that I could live partly on some money I already had but I also needed to make more money. I noticed where I was spending money that didn't need to be spent. No more manicures, meals out in restaurants and other non-essentials for a while. I created a budget and as much as I could, I stuck to it. Discount supermarkets were about to become my weekly stomping ground!

Next, I attended to the practical steps of starting a business by getting an ABN number, a business bank account and creating a website. I found a room one day a week in a healing centre in a suburb of Sydney where I was unknown. If I was going to *"fake it till I made it"*, it was easier to be surrounded by strangers and not people I knew! Months went by with no clients, but I filled in my time by creating promotional materials such as flyers which I dropped in at local cafes and shops. I also went over my text books and attended a Reiki course and was practising Reiki on myself.

Every Wednesday I would turn up at the practice room, looking like the counsellor I hoped to be, gazing at the empty client chair. Of course I felt disheartened, and thoughts of failure became my constant companions. It all seemed futile, until the phone rang. That one phone call was the beginning of my journey to success.

The commitment to starting my business and taking the necessary action, even though I was riddled with self-doubt, did eventually pay off. What I learned was:

1. Commit to what you want
2. Ensure you're financially safe
3. Take the necessary actions that support that vision
4. Don't expect to become an overnight success
5. Patience obtains all things.

Let us explore these five points.

1. Commit to What You Want

Starting your own business and finding the success you desire is a process; it is a growth journey in and of itself. The Universe will provide all that you need along the way as long as you:

Have a deep desire to make it work - It's a good idea to ask yourself just how much you want this venture to work. Do you have a strong enough "Why"? As I've already said, deep desire or passion is the correct vibration through which all things manifest. Feelings of inspiration, excitement, joy and enthusiasm all emanate from deep desire.

Have the faith and belief that it can ultimately work - This doesn't mean that you have to 100 percent believe that this is all going to work out easily. It doesn't mean that you don't have blind spots, self-doubt and fear. This is all quite normal. But it does mean that you are willing to have faith that it will eventually lead to success, even if you don't know how yet.

Hold a clear definite vision in your consciousness - Begin with the end in mind. Having a visual picture or movie in your mind that encapsulates your vision of success is a powerful way to manifest. By doing this, you are giving the Universe your vision. If you visualise regularly your ideal outcome until you are in the feeling place of it, you create a vibration that draws your vision to you and you to it. The Universe will go about orchestrating everything that needs to happen so as to create this. This is the **Universal Law of Attraction.**

Take aligned action - Commitment requires action. Action says to the Universe "I'm serious about this", and then the Universe takes you seriously. This is the **Universal Law of Action**. It's important to know what you want and to dream of what you want, but action is also a necessary part of the equation. Inspired action is the best form of action. Action that is uninspiring will not contain the same energy. You don't need to scare yourself by taking on too much. Just take a step towards what it is you want. When that step works out, take another, and then another, always heading towards what you want, and not away from what you want.

Let go of all doubt and disbelief as they arise - Doubt and disbelief WILL arise, because humans do not believe possible what they haven't yet experienced. We are all in a process of shedding old self-limiting beliefs and programming, and so by default we may fall into doubt and disbelief on a regular basis when first we walk this new path.

Be kind and loving to yourself - It is inevitable that as you take this journey, you will be faced over and over again with yourself, your limiting beliefs, your old patterns and your fears. Be willing to be compassionate with yourself as you grow and learn. Love is the only vibration that heals.

Have patience and stay determined - Our ego likes to force its own idea of timing onto everything, to our detriment. Stay aware that the timing of all things is up to the Universe, and not you. When you allow Universal timing to take place, all is perfect and well. Be patient and peaceful and yet also stay determined that all will work out. Just as a rose blooms, so shall your business in divine and perfect timing. This is the **Universal Law of Timing**.

2. Ensure You're Financially Safe

Starting a business can bring up a lot of financial fear. Most of us have become used to particular forms of income. When we were children, we were financially supported by our parents or caregivers. When we grew up, most of us became employed, and we've been used to receiving a regular payment from the organisation we work for. Being paid by an employer is predictable, and therefore it feels safe. The ego loves predictability!

When starting a new business, there is no guarantee when the business will begin to make money. One of the most common reasons that we enforce false timelines on the progress of our business is the need to make enough money from the business as soon as possible, so as to support ourselves. However, the fear of not having enough money can interfere with the love and purpose we feel for what we do. Having another form of income or finance available is essential in the early days of your business.

Emma's Story - Not making a financial plan

Emma had studied naturopathy and had wanted to go into her own business for many years. She decided one day that she would do it, without making financial considerations. She came to see me six months after leaving her job. She had invested a lot of time and money in her business but there were few clients and very little income. The worse things became, the more fearful she became, and so the worse things became. When fear creeps in, business creeps out. She couldn't afford to keep going. I asked her if she had made a financial plan when she decided to leave her job and start her own business.

"No," Emma replied *"I had assumed that if I took the plunge and followed my calling, it would all work out. Isn't that what a lot of the spiritual teachers tell us?"*

Emma is not the only client I have met who has made this assumption based on a very simplistic idea. It's a lovely thought that if we jump into the unknown wholeheartedly full of purpose, everything will fall into place. However, we all have self-limiting beliefs and old conditioning that won't become apparent until we make the shift. Together, Emma and I worked out a plan of how she could keep her business going while also working at something else to make enough money to stay afloat.

It is for this reason, it's important to ensure that you are financially safe. Our first chakra, or base chakra, is where we hold our primary needs - food and shelter ensure our survival. This means having enough money to live on or enough regular income for at least the first two years of your new business.

Some people are in the favourable position of having financial back-up, such as a spouse or partner who supports them, a sum of money already available to them such as savings, a divorce settlement or a redundancy payout. Others may seek a business loan from a bank or a financial backer. Even if you are in this position however, it can feel unsettling to watch your initial sum of money dwindle without seeing an income come in. If this is the case for you, see that sum of money as being there as the necessary foundational money that you need for now, and have faith that when the time is right, the tide will come back in and your business WILL make money.

Of course not everyone is in this position. You may need to stay employed in the early stages of starting your business. If so, choose a job that will not rob you of all your time and energy. Do not choose a job where you have to work excessively long hours, or a job that creates anxiety and stress. Let go of the need for a "status" position which will inevitably take up time and energy.

Tom's Story - Letting go of a draining job

Tom was a lawyer who didn't want to be a lawyer anymore, so he followed his passion and created an online business selling used musical instruments while trying to maintain his career in law.

"I'm exhausted," he told me. *"This job takes up all my time and energy and it's emotionally draining as well. I don't have enough time or energy to focus on my business and I really don't want to be there, but I need the money to keep the roof over my head and my new business going."*

I asked him if he'd consider doing something different to bring in an income, even if it wasn't bringing in his current salary. Tom realised that he was holding onto his career in law not just for the money, but because it gave him a sense of success and identity (even if he did hate it!). Eventually Tom recognised he could let this go, and made some significant changes. He became a barista in a coffee shop, making coffee from 7 am to 3 pm five days a week, and he moved to a smaller, less expensive apartment. He now had the time and energy to put into his online business, as well as follow his true passion which was playing live gigs.

Expecting your business to make you money immediately is unrealistic. Look to nature to appreciate the way things grow. An oak tree starts out as an acorn, and that acorn takes time to germinate and to grow a shoot. It takes 15 to 20 years to become a sapling, and 50 years before it is a mature tree that produces acorns. Of course the growth of your business will not take as long as this, but I am using the oak tree as a metaphor to illustrate an important point.

When you have enough income coming in from another source, you won't taint your business with the vibration of fear, anxiety and lack. Instead, you fill it with love and passion, knowing that you are safe and you already have enough to live on. You don't want or need to be desperate for business. You can now focus on love, passion and purpose. In time, you will be able to let go of your old form of income, as your business blossoms and creates more and more money.

Mandy's Story - Working with the Universe

Mandy wanted to start a life coaching practice, but couldn't see how it could ever happen. She had a mortgage to pay and needed her job in a bank to keep the roof over her head. Each day she would visualise herself doing her coaching work and then surrender her desire and the vision to the Universe.

Within three months, the bank began making some positions redundant and giving redundancy payouts. She enquired as to whether or not her position would be made redundant, but was told that it wouldn't be. Although she felt disappointed, she continued to surrender her desire and vision to the Universe and three months later she was offered a redundancy package which was equivalent to two years' salary. This was enough to support her for two years while she created and built up her coaching practice. Mandy is now a highly successful life coach.

My "in-between" job

After realising I never wanted to work for an organisation again, I meditated and contemplated on what I could do to bring in an income while my business was in its infancy. I decided to do babysitting, as it worked well with my family of three teenage boys who were becoming independent. I put an ad on the notice board of a local supermarket and within days I had my first regular job - caring for a young boy after school. From this work came word of mouth babysitting referrals, and I felt blessed to be doing work I enjoyed that was flexible.

3. Take the Necessary Actions that Support Your Vision

Some practical steps for the beginner in business are:

a. Create a financial plan, ensuring you have enough money or regular form of income to live on before you begin.

b. Procure an Australian Business Number (ABN) if you live in Australia, or the equivalent if you live in another country.

c. Set up a business bank account - even if you do not technically need one, having a separate business bank account makes it easier for record-keeping and tax purposes.

d. Create a business name and logo - it's important to do this early on as the business name and logo will go on your website, business cards and all future stationery. Changing a logo later on takes time and money.

e. Create a website - having a website and email address is the modern-day equivalent of having a business card. Every business has one and you need a space for people to find out about you and your products or services, and how to contact you.

f. Create business cards even if you think they are an antiquated idea. There will be opportunities where they will still be needed.

g. Seek business premises if needed.

h. Visualise your ideal result for your business.

4. Don't Expect to Become an Overnight Success

Many people believe that their business will take off immediately, and then experience feelings of failure and shame when it doesn't turn out as they planned. I believe we must all do a spiritual apprenticeship - that is, we get tested. The Universe tests our faith and commitment and if we pass that test, it then sends us opportunities, but these opportunities are not necessarily what the ego wanted or planned for. It may be doing your work at a discounted rate for a time or even doing it on a voluntary basis until you get paying clients.

It's important to remember that not everyone makes money immediately when they start a new business. Many businesses take time to build. For me and many of my clients I have witnessed the same phenomena over and over again. At the beginning there is a period of commitment and work where it may appear that you aren't making any progress. You may be putting a lot of effort in and not getting much back, but in truth you are sowing seeds that are going to take a while to germinate.

Thoughts of doubt may appear. The ego mind will have you believe that you have to push and struggle and force to

MAKE this happen. In this "sowing period" however, we are laying the foundations for the future. The Universe is testing our resolve, and asking us:

- *How much do you really want this?*
- *How committed are you?*
- *What are you prepared to give up for it?*
- *Are you willing to keep going, even without getting anything in return?*

5. Patience Obtains All Things

This is your spiritual apprenticeship. Inbuilt into everything that you REALLY WANT are challenges along the path to getting it. Do not fall for the lie that says *"If you're meant to have it, it will all fall into your lap."* That really is a myth! The truth is that for anything you truly desire, you must clear the way to getting it. There are no shortcuts to anything worth having.

Divine timing is a concept that many of us find difficult to accept. We live in a world of egoic timing - enforced timelines and deadlines, diaries, goals and time pressures. **The Universal Law of Divine Timing** is a law that deems "Thy timing and not my timing."

When we live by this law, we allow organic timing to take place and let go of false timing. The Universe is a Divine Intelligence that knows the ideal timing of everything. When we allow this law to rule, and not our ego mind, our manifestation will be perfect. If however, we push for timing that is out of alignment with our highest good, we may manifest something too soon, and we may not have the other energetic elements in place to support and sustain what we create. It can be frustrating and disheartening to manifest something that we are not ready for, because it will come in and it will go out again.

Embrace The Universal Law of Surrender

The Universal Law of Surrender is a powerful law that requires "handing over" our hopes and dreams to the Divine Intelligence. We can also surrender our feelings of impatience, frustration, hopelessness or whatever it is we feel when things don't turn out as we hope. We can then be at peace, knowing that the Universe is in charge of all manifestations.

Commitment and action led to my first miracle

After renting a room one day a week and not seeing any clients come through the door for at least the first four months, I received a phone call. A salesperson from an online deal company had found my flyer and wanted to know if I would be willing to do a Reiki deal. While I would be doing reiki sessions for a very small sum of money, it was a great way of getting people through the door and practising my healing work. We ran the deal and within a few days we sold over 500 reiki vouchers.

The money I received from the deal company was enough to rent a full time room for three months. I worked diligently and I certainly learned a lot in that three months. I was undertaking my spiritual apprenticeship! My babysitting work was over! I was surprised how many people wanted to come back and pay full-price for reiki and counselling.

Until one is committed, there is hesitancy, the chance to draw back, always ineffectiveness.

Concerning all acts of initiative and creation, there is one elementary truth, the ignorance of which kills countless ideas and splendid plans; that the moment one commits oneself, then Providence moves too.

All sorts of things occur to help one that would never otherwise have occurred. A whole stream of events issues from the decision, raising in one's favour all manner of unforeseen incidents and meetings and material assistance, which no man would have dreamed would have come his way.

Scottish Himalayan Expedition

Crafting Your Spiritual Business Plan

Exercise 4 - Journaling

Take some time to contemplate and journal by answering the following questions. Write as much or as little as you wish.

Why do I want this?

What are the likely initial costs in setting up my business?

What are my monthly living costs?

- Rent or home repayment
- Food
- Bills
- Petrol or transport costs
- Personal items
- Entertainment
- Other

In what ways can I cut down my living costs?

In what ways can I ensure I have enough money to live on over the next few years?

What actions can I take now towards starting or continuing my business?

Exercise 5 - A Prayer of Commitment

Be still and allow yourself to feel quiet and calm.

Say the following prayer to the Universe:

I surrender to You my deep desire for this business to work and succeed.
I surrender to you all self-doubt.
I surrender all egoic thoughts of success.
I surrender all impatience
Thank You for providing we with all that I need.
And for taking my vision to its highest possibility.

Chapter 3
The Magic of Getting There

The journey to becoming soulfully successful is a sacred healing process

When you decide to work for yourself, you have no idea of what you're getting yourself into. Put another way, this is the beginning of a journey into worlds you do not yet know. The unknown is the field of infinite possibilities - it is mysterious, exciting and transformational. It is inevitable that desiring something beyond what you have now will expand you and your world.

This is **The Universal Law of Pure Potential** - you are pure potential. Within you exists infinite possibilities, even if your limited ego mind tells you otherwise. The intention to work for yourself and to want to be successful breaks you out of an old mould and opens you up to expand into the new. You have talents and abilities within you that you don't even know you have yet. **The Universal Law of Perpetual Transmutation of Energy** deems that you have all the power within you to transform yourself and your circumstances.

Focus on the journey, and not the destination

Beware the ego and its impatience. The ego wants to be "over there" where the end goal is; it doesn't want to be "here" in the unknown and in the process. But please understand that getting there is a process. So why not enjoy the process? Become aware of whenever your ego mind is feeding you thoughts of impatience, fear and lack such as:

- I should have more clients by now
- I should have made more money by now
- I'm never going to get there
- That person is doing better than I am
- Things aren't going according to plan
- I don't have enough time
- I don't have enough clients
- I don't have enough followers
- I don't have enough resources
- I don't have enough money.

This list could go on for pages, but I'm sure you get what I'm saying. The ego mind perceives life through the lens of "not enough".

Abundance Vs. Scarcity

The truth is that no matter what your circumstances, the power is within you to be successful. **The Universal Law of Abundance** deems that you have within you everything required to make your earthly incarnation a paradise if you choose to accept the truth that abundance is your divine birthright. We live in a Universe of abundance, although the majority of those populating our planet currently view it as a Universe of scarcity - a scarcity of time, resources, money, love and anything else you can think of. By default, our minds are programmed to think in terms of lack and not abundance, so have compassion for yourself if you fall into this mode of thinking from time to time, or even more often!

Challenges and Miracles

There's also another Universal Law known as **The Universal Law of Challenges**, and this law deems that we WILL be sent challenges throughout our lives. Why? Because we are here to transform and grow, and we will only transform and grow through challenges. By being faced with a challenge and seeking resolution, we grow and we become a higher and lighter version of ourselves.

The path to success is an interesting blend of both miracles and challenges. The miracles are evidence that you are connected and in flow. The challenges are showing you where you need to grow. All of us have limiting beliefs from our upbringing, our family, our ancestors and even our past lives. We live in a world created by the sum total of everyone's consciousness, so we are constantly being bombarded with messages of limitation and fear - from the media, the government, and even from people we know and love.

Acceptance

For this reason, we must learn to accept both the miracles AND the challenges as a loving gift from the Universe. Problems and challenges are an opportunity for us to grow. **The Universal Law of Acceptance** tells us that that which we accept has the power to change, but that which we resist persists. Challenges are inbuilt into every life to ensure our growth and transformation. When we accept them, we work with them, and not against them. By accepting everything that happens to us, whether we judge it as positive or negative, good or bad, we acknowledge it is all in our highest good, given to us by a loving Universe. The challenges are for our growth and learning, and the miracles are our rewards for divinely right thinking.

Thoughts are powerful energy forms

Whenever you experience challenges or problems in your business, pay attention to your thoughts. It's not what happens to you or your business that's the problem; it's what you THINK about what happens to you and your business that's the problem. Thoughts are powerful energy forms that create a vibration.

Our thoughts can only ever come from two places - love or fear. And our thoughts can only be of two vibrations - abundance or lack. Our thoughts are always going in one direction or another -

- Love or fear
- Abundance or lack

- Expansion or contraction.

If you're feeling pessimistic, hopeless or negative about yourself or your business, I can guarantee you it's because you're thinking in terms of fear and lack. These thoughts aren't true and they won't serve you. If you find yourself constantly thinking in terms of fear and lack, it isn't your fault. There is an underlying reason for why this is happening - and the reason is limiting beliefs.

In the coming three chapters, we will be delving deeply into these beliefs - about ourselves, about money and about life in general, and shining a light on all that is holding you back from divinely right thinking and manifesting your true success.

Moving from fear to love

The Universe loves you. It created you and it only ever wants what is best for you. The Universe wants you to transform to the highest version of yourself. So even if things are happening that bring up fear in the form of negative emotions, there is always a loving reason behind it, even if you can't see that yet. When we choose to see all that happens through the filter of love and not fear, it takes on a whole new meaning.

Fear exists to some extent in all of us. If you are feeling fear or a sense of lack in any area of your life, you are not alone. It's normal and it's human to have fear, and to believe in lack. Fearing that there's not going to be enough is a protective mechanism of the ego that keeps us vigilant.

Fear isn't something we can push away or wish away. Telling yourself *"I shouldn't feel this way"* or *"I'm not going to feel this way"* is pointless and self-sabotaging. The only way to conquer our fear is to acknowledge it and accept it. Acceptance is love in action. Acceptance creates a vibration that connects us to the Universal Source. Accepting our fear is the first step in moving towards love and abundance.

An important realisation on my journey

When I started my business, I felt divinely guided to do what I wished to do and I felt grateful that I'd discovered my purpose. I felt grateful for the miracle of the 500 reiki deals. But that's where my spiritual connection ended. I thought of the Universe as saying to me:

"OK, I've guided you to your purpose and what you need to do, so get on with it. My job is done".

I didn't understand that it would provide ALL that I needed in every moment of time if I kept my intentions.

The Reiki deals were beginning to come to an end and while I had paying clients, there weren't enough to provide me with enough income. I defaulted into "lack" thinking, and I began to think fearful thoughts. I needed to manifest more business. I was about to learn even more about the ingenuity of the Universe and a whole lot more about myself!

I proactively began to meditate and pray each day. As I accepted all as it was, I became aware that this quieter phase was a gift and not a loss. I began to sense that my path may not be as a traditional counsellor. More and more I felt guided to follow my heart. I had been gaining a lot of insights and healing knowledge, and I felt inspired to write my first book Five Steps to Finding Love, based on the work I had been doing with the women who were coming to see me who were looking for a loving relationship.

Once I was clear on my intention, the person I needed to help me arrived at my practice door! Referred to me for Reiki by my client Veronica, her friend Daniel didn't resonate with Reiki that much, but he had just the skills I needed to help me publish and market my first book. Daniel became an important part of my business for many years, as he had knowledge and skills I didn't have. When the book was published, I was surprised by how many people wanted to buy it and even more surprised by how many more people were coming to see me.

For years I had been reading the tarot for myself and friends, but had never considered it to be a "bona fide" modality to use as a counsellor and reiki practitioner. I had come to know a healing practitioner called Jacqui who rented a room in the same building as me. She asked me to do a reading for her which she found helpful, and she suggested I bring it into my practice to help my clients. I felt resistant, fearing judgment and not being taken seriously. There is still so much judgment and misunderstanding about the tarot, but I trusted her suggestion, and her guidance was right. I began to draw to me people who needed life path guidance.

A year later, during a period of financial stress, another inspiration dropped in during a prayer and meditation session, to teach Reiki. Yet again, I was sent just the person I needed at the time. I met a Reiki Master who wanted to learn how to read the tarot. We agreed on a contra-deal - she would teach and attune me to Reiki 3 and I would teach her to read the tarot. Within weeks I was teaching groups. My income went up considerably and so did my level of fulfilment and purpose.

On every step of the path, the Universe sent me what I needed. The Universe sent me the means to find the resources I needed to start my business, it sent me new ideas and inspirations to keep going, it sent me the perfect people who were helpful and inspirational at the right time, and eventually it sent me more clients and more money.

And believe me, if you feel a sense of inspiration and excitement about your business, then you will receive Universal help too. Universal connection is the way! You are always supported by a loving Universe. Everything that happens to us is created by a loving Universe, even the so-called negative stuff. Help is all around you when you decide to live your purpose. You are not alone. The Universe is wanting to work with you and to help you.

Divine Synchronicity

Along this journey, I have learned that the way to success is through *Thy way* and not *My way* - the way of the Universe, not the way of my ego. I have met many people who have been "the right people at the right time." Some have been people who have come to help me in my business such as Daniel and my current Assistant Extraordinaire Ben; some have offered me opportunities such as guest speaking, interviews and podcasts, others have been healers and coaches who have helped me at just the right moment in time in just the right way, some have been friends who have given me ideas, guidance and encouragement; others still have recommended or even given me a book that I greatly benefitted from reading. Many times the books found me in random ways. I have been shown over and over again that life contains no accidents. If one remains open, aware and flexible, one is able to see the opportunity and seize it.

Flexibility

Be prepared that your original vision you had for yourself may change or alter as you grow and get to know yourself more. Mine certainly did. I went from my original intention of being a counsellor to becoming an energy healer and intuitive life path guide, an author and a teacher. Through surrender, I have been shown the way. And it really has been Thy Way and not My Way. Thy Way is the way!

Establishing a Divine Connection

You are a co-creator. There is no need to do this journey alone. In fact if you do, it's going to be a lot harder and less joyful than if you team up with the Light. The Source is the Supreme Intelligence and when you connect with the Source, you have all the clarity, the intelligence and the manifesting power that you need. You also have the ability to know when divine synchronicity is at work. However, most of us default into the disconnected ego self unless we put regular practices in place to stay connected. The ways that have worked best for me have been meditation, journaling, affirmations and prayer. I do these daily and they have made all the difference to me and my business. We are all unique and so it's important to find a way that resonates with you. Here are a few suggestions:

- Meditation
- Prayer
- Yoga
- Mindful walking
- Quiet reflective time alone
- Time alone in nature
- Journaling
- Reading books that expand mind and spirit
- Affirmations
- Creative pursuits.

I would suggest that if you want to strengthen your connection to the Universe, make your spiritual practices little and often, as opposed to big and occasional. Not that big and occasional are out of the question - by all means if you feel compelled to go on a retreat or attend a self development conference, you must! Just remember however, that a daily practice when you get home is still necessary. I have provided a simple meditation practice in the back of this book.

Harry's Story - From connected to disconnected to connected again!

Harry had recently returned from South America when he came to see me. Feeling flat and disheartened, he shared with me that he had been on a long shamanic retreat and had come back to Australia feeling excited because, while on his retreat, he had a vision about his purpose and the business he wished to create. He had started out feeling hopeful and energetic but within weeks he was floundering, feeling unmotivated and riddled with self-doubt. I asked him if he had been keeping up any spiritual practices since coming home from his spiritual sabbatical, and the answer was no.

"Why not?" I asked.

Harry sat with the question and replied *"My experiences in South America were so amazing, that it feels boring and uninspiring to sit on my own to meditate."*

I understood. Retreats can be life-changing experiences - especially if they involve taking the hallucinatory substance ayahuasca, and communing in a beautiful rainforest with others also on a spiritual journey, but these peak experiences can become addictive unless we can see them for what they are. Everyday life can appear drab when reality inevitably shows up. Harry had gone from being super-connected to completely disconnected!

I explained to him that the connection he felt in South America is also possible here, but only he could make it happen. He began a daily morning meditation practice and he followed my suggestion to visualise the divine result he wanted for his business at the end of each meditation and then give thanks and surrender. Combined with daily actions, Harry began to get traction, and as he felt a sense of movement forward into his vision, he began to feel more hopeful and more powerful. While he wasn't experiencing the ecstasy he felt in South America, he was moving peacefully and evermore joyfully into his future success.

You are a co-creator

The Universal Law of Surrender is a powerful Universal law. Whatever we wish to manifest, we hand over to the Supreme Intelligence which knows exactly how to create what we want. By incorporating this law with the **Universal Law of Action**, we then become a co-creator.

Surrender your long-term vision to the Universe as you take action on your short term goals. This way, you are moving forward perfectly, while remembering the **Universal Law of Divine Timing** - *Thy* timing and not *My* timing.

Daily tasks

A few years ago I read these wise words:

Successful people do the things that unsuccessful people aren't prepared to do.

This really is true. In order to get to the end game, there are going to be tasks that we may not want to do, but have to do. If there are tasks that you feel unmotivated to do, or even repelled by, ask yourself:

- How do I feel about this task?
- What don't I like about this task?
- How can I make this task more enjoyable?

In the words of Mary Poppins, *"In every task that must be done, there is an element of fun. You find the fun, and snap! The job's a game."*

I have found that giving myself regular rewards throughout difficult tasks has worked well. If a particular task requires expertise I do not have or I do not have the time to acquire, handing the task to an expert has been a good decision.

Signs and Guidance

Just as the right people and opportunities come our way, often we are sent signs and guidance. Even before I began my business, I was aware that dragonflies were a powerful symbol that kept showing up for me during times of change. They symbolise for me that I am transforming and that I'm on the right track with the changes I'm making. Butterflies represent transformation, but for me they have often shown up as a sign of new beginnings.

Numbers are also symbolic, especially double and triple numbers such as 11, 111, 22, 222, 33 and 333 and so on. In general, numbers symbolise growing awareness and consciousness but they can also symbolise the presence of angels and Higher Beings and are confirmation of whatever it is you're thinking or choosing at the time.

At times I've had some very direct messages from the Universe, such as the time when I was feeling disheartened and full of self-doubt, and I received in my letterbox a large sign on the back of a junk mail envelope that read 'STAY DETERMINED". Take time each day to become aware of your surroundings and stay open to signs and guidance. You will be amazed at how often you are sent messages from Source.

I have weapons ye know not of!

I have ways ye know not of!

I have channels ye know not of!

Mysterious weapons, mysterious ways, mysterious channels!

For God works in mysterious ways, his wonders to perform.

The trouble with most people is that they want to know the way and the channels beforehand.

They want to tell Supreme Intelligence just how their prayers should be answered.

They do not trust the wisdom and ingenuity of God.

They pray, giving Infinite Intelligence definite directions how to work, thereby limiting the Holy One of Israel.

Florence Scovel Shinn

Crafting Your Spiritual Business Plan

Exercise 6 - Journaling

Take some time to contemplate and journal by answering the following questions. Write as much or as little as you wish.

What thoughts do I have that are based on fear or lack? (write as many as come up for you)

What am I struggling to accept?

What do I see as my current challenges?

What are the qualities I need to develop in myself so as to get through these challenges?

Are there any tasks I don't want to do but have to do?

In what ways can I create more enjoyment in the doing of these tasks?

In what way or ways can I strengthen my Universal connection each day?

- Meditation
- Prayer

- Yoga
- Mindful walking
- Quiet reflective time alone
- Time alone in nature
- Journaling
- Reading books that expand mind and spirit
- Affirmations
- Creative pursuits.

Have I experienced any of the following?

- Divine Synchronicity
- Universal Signs and Guidance

Exercise 7 - A Daily Prayer of Surrender and Presence

Be still and allow yourself to feel quiet and calm. Say the following prayer to the Universe:

I surrender to You this day.
I surrender to you my challenges, my worries and my fears.
May they all be resolved in Divine and perfect timing.
May today I honour my journey and know
That I am exactly where I need to be.
May I achieve each task with grace and ease.
May I be open to every gift you send me
And open to Your signs and guidance.
Thank You.

Chapter 4
Transform Your Relationship with Yourself

What you believe about yourself will either expand or limit your success

Everything that happens to us and around us is a mirror of what we believe about ourselves. Everything that is happening or not happening in your business is a mirror of what you believe about yourself. You are your business! **The Universal Law of Belief** deems that whatever we believe we create. If you believe that you're not good enough, then your business will never be good enough. If you believe you're not important, your business won't ever become important.

If you believe you don't deserve, then you can be sure that not much business is going to be happening. If any of these beliefs sound like yours, you are not alone, and it's not your fault. Many of the limiting beliefs we have about ourselves were formed in our earliest years, and some go even further back to our ancestors whose imprints still exist in our DNA.

The good news is that we can move beyond self-limiting beliefs if we:

- Locate the belief
- Examine the belief
- Reprogram a new belief.

And that's exactly what I'm going to be teaching you to do in this chapter. Do not underestimate the importance of this. Unless we wake up and take responsibility for our self beliefs, and know that we have the power to change them and therefore change our reality, we will keep perpetuating the same old reality.

Some of our beliefs about ourselves we may be consciously aware of and some we may hold at the subconscious or even unconscious level. Our energy field contains traumas and old programming not just from this life, but from our ancestors' lives and even past lives. I'd like to share with you some of the most common self-limiting beliefs that hold people back when it comes to being successful in business (or in any other area of their life for that matter):

- I'm not good enough
- I'm not worthy or deserving
- I don't have what it takes
- I can't - I'm stupid / I'm not creative
- I'm inferior / not important
- I'm not wanted

- People will betray me or let me down
- I must put other people before myself
- I'm bound to fail
- If things don't go the way I want them to, it means I'm a failure
- I'm VERY worthy, deserving and important
- People should do what I expect them to do.

Let me now share with you an example of how each of these beliefs have played out in my clients' lives or in my own life, and some affirmations to reprogram a new belief.

Tony's story - I'm not good enough

Tony had a great business idea but he dreaded making proposals and dealing with potential clients. He believed in the product he'd created, but he didn't believe that he was good enough to sell it. The very thought of "selling" made him recoil.

"I don't believe that anyone would want to buy my product," said Tony *"when there are plenty of others out there."*

Tony had fallen into the competitive mindset, as opposed to focussing on his unique selling proposition (I will be sharing more with you about marketing in Chapter 7). I told Tony that there were always going to be competitors out there, but that each of us is unique, which makes our product unique. His job was to focus on what the product had to give, and not on what other products were out there. Tony had to stay in his own lane!

We drilled a little further to discover that Tony didn't feel good enough. He was relieved when I assured him that this is the most common belief - most of us to some extent don't believe we're good enough, and when we're attempting for the first time to sell our services or products, we can suffer from "impostor syndrome."

I shared with him the old Marx Brothers joke *"Who would want to belong to a club who had me for a member?"* Humour can be very healing! I also shared with him some good advice from my one-day counselling practice seminar - *"Fake it till you make it."*

Affirmations

I now release the past and I am willing to know that I am good enough.

My products and services are good enough.

People are in need of my products and services.

Debbie's story - I don't deserve

Even though Debbie had been in business for five years as a tutor, she had come to see me because she was struggling financially and only "just got by." (I will be sharing a lot more about money with you in the next chapter). Not long into our conversation, she revealed that she gave discounts to almost every one of her students because she believed that they couldn't afford her full rate. Her anger was obvious when she shared with me that other tutors not only charged full rate, but they also had more students than she had.

"Why would this be? I just don't understand," she said.

"Could it be that those other tutors feel that they deserve the full rate and you don't?" I asked. *"And could it be that because they feel deserving, they are open to receiving more?"*

Debbie blinked as she digested this idea, but went on to defend her undeserving self.

"I'm trying to do right by my students," she said.

"At the cost of doing right by you." I asked if she thought her rate was a reasonable one and she said yes.

"Debbie, you are worthy and deserving of the full rate you have set. Your job is to now stick to this rate. If a student cannot afford you, they will have to find another tutor."

"But who will teach them?" asked Debbie.

"Someone who is doing what you're doing right now!"

Debbie kept charging her current students at the discounted rate, but she began charging all new students at the full rate. Not only did Debbie's income improve; she began to attract more students and not less.

Affirmations

I now release the past and I am willing to know that I am worthy and deserving.

I am worthy and deserving of being paid well for my services.

Tim's story - I don't have what it takes

When I met Tim, he was exhausted from working in sales for a large international financial organisation, passionless about the products he was required to sell and tired from having to achieve targets every quarter.

I'd asked Tim my golden question:

"If a fairy waved her magic wand over you tonight as you slept, and you could wake up doing what you'd really love to do, what would it be?"

"I'd love to restore old things and have a shop full of interesting recycled stuff, but I can't see how that could ever happen. I wouldn't know the first thing about being in my own business."

"Just because you don't know the first thing doesn't mean that you don't have all the resources within you to find out and maybe even do it."

I told Tim that you don't need to know everything there is to know immediately. You learn as you go. And whatsmore, he would find he had further skills and talents that he may not even be aware of yet. We all do; but we've got to step into the unknown to find them.

A light bulb went on for Tim. He had mistaken the "unknown" for a dark and limited place, as opposed to the field of infinite possibilities.

Affirmations

I have all the resources within me to start and succeed.

The unknown is the field of infinite possibilities within me.

I have everything it takes to succeed.

Leah's story - I can't

Leah had a very successful online jewellery business and was asked to speak at a forum for online entrepreneurs. This was a great opportunity for Leah but the thought of speaking in public crippled her with fear.

"I can't get up in front of all those people," she said.

I asked her to tell me the first or worst time she experienced a fear of public speaking. Leah recalled being extremely shy at school and becoming tongue tied during a talk to the class and everyone laughing at her.

We did some trauma release work together and Leah was beginning to realise that she could do this.

Affirmations

I now release the past and I am willing to know that I can.

I can move beyond old limitations.

I can do all that I need to do to reach my full potential.

Ben's story - I'm inferior / not important

Ben was a cafe owner and his business was struggling. Not long after opening, another cafe opened nearby and it pained Ben to see that people flocked to the cafe across the road and not to his. During the course of our conversation, Ben shared with me that it reminded him of how he felt growing up. His older brother Will was a high achiever at school and his parents and teachers often espoused the dreaded remark *"Why can't you be more like Will?"*

Throughout his life, Ben felt inferior to his older brother and not important. So it wasn't surprising that Ben was now re-enacting a similar scenario in business, where he felt that he and his business were inferior and not important. I shared with Ben that when we believe that we (and therefore our business) are unimportant or inferior, we will unconsciously create a business that looks and feels unimportant and inferior.

We did some EFT and NLP around feeling important, and when Ben's vibration lifted, he reported to me within a week that he had new inspirations for food and decor for the cafe. Business is now booming.

Affirmations

I now release the past and am willing to know that I am important and equal to anyone else.

I am important and my business is important.

My story - I'm not wanted

I had no idea that on a deep level I held the belief *"I'm not wanted"*. This was revealed to me in a kinesiology session just a few years after I had begun my business. This belief began when I was in my mother's womb. My father wasn't ready for a second child. Of course I know he wants me now and I'm so glad that my Dad and I enjoy a great relationship, but this didn't prevent me from being wounded at the time and taking that wound with me throughout my life, until it was ready to reveal itself to me.

This belief was affecting my business in its early days. Business would flow and then it would stop, because deep down I believed I wasn't wanted or wouldn't be wanted eventually. When I became aware of this belief and cleared it, business began to flow consistently..

Affirmations

I now release the past and I am willing to know that I am wanted.

I am wanted by my clients.

I am wanted by the Universe.

Sylvia's story - people will betray me or let me down

Sylvia was an interior designer who was asked to decorate the home of a client while she was travelling overseas. They stayed in communication throughout the job and Sylvia regularly sent photos of the interior renovation which the client loved. So it came as a very unpleasant surprise to Sylvia when the client flew into a rage on her return from overseas and told Sylvia that she hated the new decor. The client demanded her money back or she would sue. Sylvia decided to pursue the matter legally. When we met, she was understandably in a state of high anxiety.

During our session together, I took Sylvia through a process called a Soul Truth Healing and we discovered that there was a past life trauma in her energy field where Sylvia had been falsely accused of a crime and condemned to death. At a deep level she was still holding the belief that was formed in that past life that people would falsely accuse her and condemn her. On reflection she realised that she had experienced similar scenarios in the past. We cleared the old energy and eventually the case was dropped. No such scenario has since played out for Sylvia.

Affirmations

I now release the past and I am willing to know that people are trustworthy.

I attract trustworthy and honest people into my life.

My business attracts trustworthy and honest people.

Rachel's story - I must put other people before myself

Rachel had been wanting to start her own business for quite some time, but there was always something in the way. She felt frustrated. When we dug deeper, the things that were standing in the way were her plans with her husband.

Rachel was perennially waiting for certain plans to come to fruition before she could "move forward" into her business - waiting to move apartments because her husband wasn't happy where they were living, waiting for her husband to get organised in the new apartment, waiting until her husband felt settled in a new job, waiting until they had an overseas trip he dearly wanted, and waiting until her husband agreed on her plans.

Rachel was putting her marriage before her purpose. Many women do this, but interestingly, not so many men do it! I suggested to Rachel that she was still believing that *"A good woman puts everyone before herself."*

I explained to Rachel that unless she started putting herself and her purpose first, she was unlikely to move forward into her business.

Of course one's primary relationship must take a high priority, but not at cost to oneself or one's purpose.

Affirmations

It is safe to be true to me and my purpose.

It is divinely right to put myself and my purpose first.

When I am true to myself, I am true to all those around me.

Elle's story - I'm bound to fail

Elle wanted to start a catering business but felt paralysed when it came to taking the necessary steps. She revealed to me that ten years before, she and her then partner went into a business together but the business failed. They had to file for bankruptcy and the relationship then ended too. As we spoke, I sensed that Elle was holding a deep sense of failure and shame about her past "mistake".

I do believe that there are no mistakes, only lessons and I shared this with her. As long as we learn the lessons from our past mistakes or failures, then we take those valuable lessons with us into the future. I asked her to reflect on everything she learned from the experience, and what she would do differently had she known what she knew now. I asked her to meet herself with compassion and not judgement. We don't know what we don't know! Life is a school through which we learn lessons from experience.

By the end of that session, Elle's energy had totally shifted. Her posture was more open, her face more joyful. I could literally see that she had released the toxic vibration of shame and failure, and replaced it with self-compassion, understanding and the willingness to move forward into a new adventure.

Affirmations:

I now release all past traumas of failures and mistakes.

I release the shame I feel about the past.

There are no mistakes, only lessons.

I lovingly learn my lessons from the past.

I forgive myself and all those involved.

I move forward with hope and optimism.

Brendon's story - If things don't go the way I want them to, it means I'm a failure

Brendon was a life coach who created a series of workshops. He came to see me, deflated and disappointed because he was finding it difficult to get enough attendees for his first workshop. Knowing that I ran workshops, he was keen to pick my brain as to how to get more "bums on seats." He also shared with me his feelings of failure and hopelessness.

I could relate to how he felt and I explained to him, as I have earlier in this book, that we've got to let go of the idea that outcomes are going to land effortlessly into our lap. If you're not getting the result you want, there is something that needs to change.

Brendon told me he was doing all he could to get people to attend his workshop - social media ads and posts, calling existing clients and even distributing brochures. He was certainly embracing the **Universal Law of Action**! But he was doing these actions in the vibration of fear and lack, coming from his sense of failure, which creates a desperate energy. I explained to him the **Universal Law of Least Resistance** - letting go of pushing, forcing and trying too hard. As with all the Universal Laws, this Law creates the vibration of love.

I suggested to Brendon that he come back to the reason as to WHY he created the workshops, and feel that sense of passion and purpose, and to connect with his mission. Brendon's marketing then took on a whole new energy. He was simply being a messenger to let those know who would benefit from his workshop.

"Don't obsess about the numbers," I told him. *"Whatever number of attendees you get, see it as perfect. From that place, you will attract more."*

And that's exactly what happened. He had four people attend his first workshop, but now Brendon has built a strong following and with each workshop he holds, the numbers get bigger.

Affirmations

I accept that things won't always go My way; they will go Thy way.

I release the belief that just because things aren't going My way, I'm a failure.

There is no failure, only feedback.

I'm bound to experience failures on my way to success.

Every failure is a learning experience.

All I do I undertake with love, purpose and optimism.

Julie's story - I'm VERY worthy, deserving and important

Julie had been a very successful recruiter who worked for a

global recruitment firm, but she was tired of working for an organisation and knew she had the ability and the contacts to go out on her own. She didn't expect, however, that clients and cash wouldn't flow that easily in the first year of her business. I shared with her the financial sacrifices I made in the early years of my business - from getting a friend to cut and colour my hair, rarely eating out at restaurants and shopping at discount supermarkets. As I spoke these words, Julie seemed angry and resentful.

"I NEED my weekly manicures and massages. And what have I got to look forward to if I can't go out with my friends for dinner?"

"Julie, that choice is yours, but realise that there is a price to pay for everything. It's unlikely to be forever, but it may be for a while."

As with most narcissistic people, Julie found it difficult coming to terms with reality. I only saw her a few times, but she eventually returned to corporate recruitment.

Affirmations

I am worthy and deserving of success.

I accept there is a price to pay for everything.

I am willing to make sacrifices in the short term so as to reap my rewards in the long term.

Sarah's Story - People should do what I expect them to do.

When I met Sarah, she came across as hard and inflexible, so I wasn't surprised that she had come to see me because she had difficulty maintaining staff at her kitchenwares store. As we spoke, it became apparent that all of Sarah's relationships were difficult - she barely spoke to her grown up kids and other family members. Sarah had high expectations of people and poor boundaries. Her need to control people had pushed them away. I suggested to her that once she had inducted her staff, she needed to step back and allow them to feel a sense of ownership in their role. Being micromanaged can feel suffocating for a staff member and blocks their natural abilities and creative flow.

Sarah shared with me several stories of how, when she let go, staff members had made mistakes or disappointed her. I suggested that in these instances, she could communicate with that person and correct the mistake, but that there was no need to constantly control and monitor.

The belief that people should do what we expect them to and the resulting need to control other people won't allow a business to flourish. It comes from a deep down inability to trust others and to trust in life. Sarah's pattern would have started when she was very young and was not going to be released easily, but we made a start.

Affirmations

I let go of the need to control other people.

I allow other people the chance to shine in their own way.

I manage, but I now no longer control.

I see and appreciate the talents and abilities of all those around me.

I choose to trust others.

I choose to trust in life.

The Self Doubter and The Self Believer

It is inevitable that at times you are going to doubt yourself. Self-doubt really is a part of the journey, but our "Self-Doubter" is only trying to protect us. When self-doubt appears, acknowledge it. Don't push it away; he or she is just a part of you.

When you start out, there is so much you don't know - you can't know! You will learn as you go along. You'll make mistakes, perhaps you already have, but mistakes are all a part of the process. As you learn from each mistake, you take the lesson with you into your future. Let go of the need to be perfect and to get it all right. This will hold you back. Be kind to yourself, for you are journeying into the unknown. The unknown can feel scary, but it is also the field of infinite possibilities.

We may have a Self-Doubter but we also have a Self-Believer, the part of ourselves who is willing to learn from mistakes, who encourages and who doesn't give up. Every challenge is showing you something you need to heal in yourself.

The Self-Doubter perceives challenges as evidence of your not being good enough in some way. Your Self-Believer perceives challenges as a sign that there is something more to learn, to heal and to grow from.

Forgiveness

Forgiving others who hurt us, betrayed us or disappointed us in the past will ensure we are free to become our best selves. **The Universal Law of Forgiveness** deems that we free up energy within ourselves when we forgive. Unforgiveness will block your heart chakra, it will block love and it will block your good from fully coming to you. Let me define forgiveness:

Forgiveness isn't condoning the other person's behaviour, but forgiveness is acceptance of what happened and who the other person is. Forgiveness doesn't necessarily mean staying in a relationship with that person or even maintaining contact. It's about consciously letting go of the resentment and other toxic emotions that you are holding that only damage you, not the other person. It's about letting go of self-righteousness, finding peace and choosing to forgive for your own sake, not for theirs.

Forgiving yourself for past mistakes is also important. If we haven't forgiven ourselves, we will be unconsciously punishing ourselves and therefore sabotaging ourselves. Everything we chose in the past we chose with the knowledge and understanding we had at the time, so every past mistake was inevitable! We were meant to make that mistake so as to learn and grow.

Self-Acceptance

Accepting yourself just the way you are is the key to being truly successful. We are all faulty. We all have wounds from our past. Not one of us is perfect. Self-acceptance is self love! It's about accepting and releasing the shame of being who we are. When we come to terms with our past by accepting it, we come to terms with ourselves now. We don't have to be perfect; we just need to be willing to grow.

"Too many people overvalue what they are not and undervalue what they are."

Malcolm S. Forbes

Crafting Your Spiritual Business Plan

Exercise 8 - Journaling

Tick or circle any of the self-limiting beliefs that feel like yours

- I'm not good enough
- I'm not worthy or deserving
- I don't have what it takes
- I can't - I'm stupid / I'm not creative
- I'm inferior / not important
- I'm not wanted
- People will betray me or let me down
- I must put other people before myself
- I'm bound to fail
- If things don't go the way I want them to, it means I'm a failure
- I'm VERY worthy, deserving and important
- People should do what I expect them to do.

For every belief you have ticked, write down the first or worst memory that manifested from or created this belief (or write as many memories as you wish).

Refer back to the healing affirmations provided in this chapter for every self-limiting belief you have, and commit to saying these affirmations at the beginning and end of every day for the next six weeks. The affirmations are also in the back of this book.

Exercise 9 - Forgiveness

Journaling - Write a list of everyone you need to forgive.

Do the following exercise for each person you need to forgive

Visualise the person before you. Ask them to show you what happened in their past which caused them to then hurt you.

Then say to the person "I am willing to forgive you."

Take some deep and cleansing breaths. As you breathe in, breathe in white healing light, and as you breathe out, consciously release any resentment, anger, sadness and powerlessness. Become aware of the pain that comes up as you consciously let it go.

Visualise yourself from this past wounding and imagine white healing light beaming through your younger self, cleansing you of past trauma and pain.

Exercise 10 - Self-Forgiveness

Journaling - Write a list of everything you need to forgive yourself for.

In what way would your Self-Believer choose to see these past mistakes?

Do the following exercise.

Imagine your Higher Self standing behind you, and they are looking down on you with pure unconditional love. Your Higher Self is the part of you that is connected to The Divine Source and knows that life is a school and that you are here to learn. Your Higher Self places their hands on your shoulders, and fills you with healing white light. As you breathe in, breathe in the light, and as you breathe out, breathe out guilt, shame, self-loathing and all toxic emotions that do not serve you.

And now connect with your heart, your centre of love, compassion and forgiveness. Say to yourself "I am willing to forgive you." Connect with a feeling of peace and compassion for yourself.

Exercise 11 - A Prayer of Self Love

Be still and allow yourself to feel quiet and calm.

Say the following prayer to the Universe:

> *I surrender to You who I am.*
> *I surrender to You every self-limiting belief.*
> *I surrender to You my wounding and my shame.*
> *I surrender to You all that isn't love within me.*
> *May I be filled with Divine Light*
> *And know the Truth of who I really am.*
> *Thank You.*

Chapter 5
Transform Your Relationship with Money

What you believe about money will either expand or limit your income

We all have a relationship with money, and if you're in business, you need to ensure it's a healthy and functional one. Money is simply an energy of exchange, and it is the most effective energy of exchange we have ever had, because when we receive money for our goods and services, we can exchange that money for anything we want. And yet, many of us have an uncomfortable relationship with money, especially women. Money is not the problem. It's our relationship with money that can be a problem - loving money too much (greed) or loving money too little (rejection) is the problem. Onto money we can project many limiting beliefs. These beliefs come from our family of origin, and behind these family beliefs is the history of our ancestors.

The Universal Law of Belief deems that whatever we believe we create, so if you believe that money is hard to come by, you will experience just that. I'd like to share with you the most common limiting beliefs that people hold around money. In the list of beliefs below, I use the word "rich" to describe a state where all your financial needs and wants are met.

- Nice people don't talk about money.
- Money doesn't grow on trees (or there is never enough money)
- There is only ever so much to go around
- You have to work very hard to make money
- You cannot do work you love AND make good money
- It's wrong to take money from people
- Money is the root of all evil
- It is virtuous to be poor
- It's not good to be rich
- Rich people are bad people
- It's not spiritual to be rich
- It's greedy to be rich
- It's wrong to focus on money
- If you focus on money, you don't care about people
- It's ONLY money

These beliefs create lack and limitation, and many of them create a deep sense of shame in our relationship with money.

Waking up to my old money story

When I began to examine my own relationship with money, I realised it was loaded with many of these beliefs. Some of them I couldn't pinpoint as to why I would believe what I did, but I realised that these were deeply imprinted in my psyche and had been handed down from generation to generation, and were a conglomerate of many old ancestral traumas. And because one of my beliefs were "nice people don't talk about money", no communication ever happened in my family around money except for awkward conversations, and therefore there was never any healing opportunity for me around my relationship with money until I went into my own business. Then my dysfunctional relationship with money became glaringly obvious!

The truth about money and abundance

Before I share with you some stories around money to demonstrate how each limiting belief can play out, I want to share with you the truth about money.

There is a never-ending flow of abundance. Look at the abundance that is present in nature - flowers, fruits and vegetables. Observe how things grow.

Abundance is your divine right. The earth will provide for you, in whatever form your life is taking now and in the future. Trusting in a loving Universe is imperative if you want to be abundant.

The Universe wants you to be rich. It's your disconnected ego mind that doesn't believe this. Being financially abundant is all part of living your full potential here on earth.

Money flows to those who can meet a need or resolve other people's problems. When we use our gifts, skills and talents to help others, we will be financially rewarded for it.

It is divinely right to receive money for goods and services. When we receive money for our goods and services, we do not leave anybody owing us and therefore create no negative karmic bond.

The vibration (feeling) of abundance creates abundance. You cannot create abundance from the vibration (feeling) of lack. Visualising/imagining an abundant life until you are in the "feeling" place of it will draw money to you.

Money is an energy that needs to flow. If you want to attract more money, you must be willing to spend some– that is why we call it "currency".

When we treat money with respect, we will attract more of it. Like anything else, money must be respected. If we waste it on unnecessary things that are not in our highest good or spend money on things that are destructive, the source will dry up. If we spend it on all that is in our highest good, the source will keep flowing and expand.

Being unnecessarily mean with money will diminish your abundance. There is a difference between being respectful of money and being mean with money. **The Universal Law**

of Giving and Receiving requires that money needs to be circulated.

The more you know about money, the more friendly you will feel towards money. Many people feel ashamed because they are not "financially literate". The world of governments, banking and finance have made it difficult for many people to understand investment terminology, tax laws and the like, but financial literacy really isn't difficult. Knowledge is power. The more willing you are to understand the world of money, the more empowered and willing to be rich you will become.

Whatever you give away returns to you manifold. Give 10 percent of your income away to a good cause (or whatever you can at present), and your abundance will soar.

By saving 10 percent of your income just for you, your abundance will grow. When you grow a nest egg for yourself, you will feel abundant, and the feeling of abundance draws to you more abundance. The old saying *"the rich get richer and the poor get poorer"* is based on this concept.

When you pay your bills joyfully the money will return to you. Never resent bills you have to pay and taxes you have to pay. Financial responsibilities are a part of the deal here of life on earth. Be grateful that you have the money to pay your bills. Resentment blocks the flow of money returning to you.

Abundance comes from the Universe. The Universe is the Source of all abundance. Your job, investment, spouse or any other way that money comes to you is simply the channel, but not the Source. You can ask the Source for what you want

– *"Ask and it is given"* – and be open to ALL the channels of abundance (even the ones you don't know exist yet!)

On the spiritual plane, there is no such thing as loss. Energy transmutes but it never disappears. If you have experienced a financial loss, remind yourself that there is no loss and declare *"I welcome in my Divine Compensation in divine and perfect timing"*. This is **The Universal Law of Divine Compensation.**

You are an energy field of unlimited potential. Even if your circumstances appear to be limited as to how you are going to have more money, you will be presented with opportunities if you stay present and open and hold firm to a vision of abundance. This is **The Universal Law of Abundance.** You have within you everything you need to create your own earthly paradise. There is no need to wait for the "ideal" or "perfect" opportunity – any opportunity that feels right is good enough. Sometimes that opportunity will lead to another and another. Follow your gut instinct.

The intuitive path is the way to your abundance. The path of "shoulds", advice from people you don't respect or who are living lives of lack or unhappiness is not the path that will create abundance.

Gratitude is the most powerful vibration there is to attract money and abundance. Every time you receive money, say a prayer of gratitude. **The Universal Law of Gratitude** deems that whatever we are grateful for will expand. If, however, you receive money and think *"is that all there is?"* you will create the vibration of lack and attract further lack.

Money is only one aspect of abundance. If you don't have much money at present, give thanks and appreciation for all that is good in your life.

You are worthy and deserving of miracles. If you need money, connect in with the Source and ask for a miracle. Have absolute faith the matter will be resolved in a perfect way, let go and trust.

When I began to understand the Universal Laws, I was able to create a loving relationship with money and transcend all the old negative programming I had around money. So let me now share with you some stories of how our negative beliefs around money can play out.

My Story - Nice people don't talk about money

It was 1970 and I was in grade two when a fellow classmate went to the front of the class for "News" and announced excitedly that her dad had just been given a pay rise and he was now earning $100 a week (well this was 1970!). The whole class was impressed. That evening at the family dinner table, I excitedly told my mother and father about my classmate's father getting a pay rise and asked out of pure curiosity:

"How much do you earn a week Daddy?"

Well you could have heard a pin drop.

"Nicky," said my mother in an icy tone *"it is very rude to talk about money and you NEVER ask anyone what they earn."*

I blushed in shame. This message was heard loud and clear and never again did I bring up such a subject. I took this message with me well into my adulthood, and would squirm whenever anyone mentioned money. When I applied for jobs, I always let my employer do the talking when it came to money. When I got married, I felt awkward when it came to discussing finances. Before I went into my own business, I devoted a lot of my time to painting. People would offer to buy my paintings, and I would feel myself contract with awkwardness. Talking about money and negotiating a price was like pulling teeth, and I would sabotage these opportunities rather than talk "money".

Affirmations

I now release the past and know it is safe to talk about money.

I release all shame around talking about money.

Money is simply an energy of exchange.

My Story - Money doesn't grow on trees (or there is never enough money)

The phrase "we can't afford it" was said regularly in my family. I recall my sister saying how much she enjoyed having tinned salmon on her sandwiches for school lunch and my mother replying *"You can't have that every day. We can't afford it!"*

When asked what I wanted for Christmas when I was seven, I told my mother of the beautiful ballerina doll that was advertised on television. She came home from a visit to the department store a few days later and told me *"You won't be getting that doll. It's far too expensive. We can't afford it."*

And I recall how I felt every time I heard those words - small, unworthy, embarrassed and ashamed. I soon learned it was better never to ask for anything than to hear those words.

There never seemed to be enough money in my family, but it wasn't my parents' fault. They had grown up in the Great Depression and the war years and had known scarcity, as did most people of that era. It was deeply imprinted into their psyche. My ancestors on both sides were first settlers who were in truth "economic refugees" escaping the Irish famine or poverty in the United Kingdom. Even though my parents actually did quite well financially eventually (both worked full time), survival mode and the fear of not enough money was never far from their minds. "Not enough" was a deeply entrenched belief.

Affirmations

I now release the past and know that there is always enough.

There always has been enough money and there always will be enough money.

I always have enough money for anything that is in my highest good.

Money flows to me effortlessly and easily.

Abundance is my Divine right.

Ollie's Story - There is only ever so much to go around & It's wrong to take money from people

Ollie had a small IT business and specialised in fixing computers and phones. He told me he felt guilty every time he charged a client, believing that he was diminishing their wealth when he was paid by them. He also resented paying his income tax every quarter, believing that the Tax Office was also diminishing his wealth.

"Ollie, you are not diminishing your clients' wealth. You are creating a fair exchange – they get their computer back fixed and ready to go, and you get money to live on. Many of your clients work for themselves, so their computer or phone is key to them creating their own wealth, so in fact you are also creating wealth for them. And as for the Tax Office, I'm sure you've heard the old saying that only two things are certain – death and taxes. Accept that taxes are a part of life and the world we currently inhabit. When you pay your taxes you are giving to the whole. Pay your taxes joyfully and the money will come back to you."

Many people have this fixed idea that there is only a certain amount of money available to anyone, and when they take money from that person, they have somehow diminished that person's wealth, but this really isn't the case. Abundance is ever-flowing. By helping someone in any way, you will ultimately add to their wealth. Whether you sell them food, cut their hair, mow their lawn or anything else. The Universe works on exchange and there is infinite abundance available to all of us. We really are all just circulating this amazing thing called money!

Affirmations

When I receive I also give.

When I give I also receive.

There is a flow of infinite abundance available to all.

My Story - You have to work very hard to make money

My family had a very strong work ethic. My parents both worked hard; Dad was an electrical foreman and mum was a nurse and midwife. We were all encouraged to work hard too, and my first 45 years were a story of hard work. As I awakened, it became very apparent to me that I was here to experience a wonderful life, and I knew that this wonderful life was not going to be created by working long hours and exhausting myself. Yes, I wanted to work, but I also wanted to enjoy every aspect of my life. When I decided to go into my own healing practice, I initially felt guilty taking people's money, because the work I was doing was fulfilling and enjoyable. Deep down, I was still programmed with the old beliefs of hardship, sacrifice and struggle. This all felt too easy!

Affirmations

I am worthy of doing work that I love.

Money comes to me easily and effortlessly as I let go of old beliefs.

Work and money are exchanged with love.

Sandi's story - You cannot do work you love *and* make good money

Sandi was a corporate consultant who had fallen out of love with the corporate world. Her passion was pottery and she spent much of her spare time at the potter's wheel and had begun to sell her creations at weekend markets.

"I'd love to do this full-time, but it would never pay all my bills."

I suggested to Sandi that underneath that statement was the belief that she couldn't do work that she loved and get paid good money for it.

"You're right! The only reason I became a consultant was because I got very good grades and my parents encouraged me to go into accounting because I'd earn good money."

"How are you with the idea that you could make just as much money doing something you loved as doing something you don't love? Eventually, that is."

"I'll need to think about that," Sandi said, but she was smiling.

Sandi sat with the idea that she really could make good money from doing something she loved, and from that place of possibility, an idea dropped in. Sandi hired a space where she could do her pottery but also teach pottery to kids. This way she created two streams of income. Very soon the parents were asking her if she could teach them too. Corporate consulting is no longer a part of Sandi's life.

Affirmations

I am worthy of doing work that I love and making good money.

I allow myself to be wealthy and happy.

Isobel's Story - Money is the root of all evil, It is virtuous to be poor, It's not good to be rich, Rich people are bad people, It's not spiritual to be rich, It's greedy to be rich

Isobel was a healer whose attitude towards money was typical of many women I have met, particularly healers. Underlying all her beliefs about money was the idea that money was bad and even dirty. I told Isobel that I couldn't see anything bad in money; it was purely a source of exchange.

"Jesus Christ didn't charge for his healings," said Isobel.

"Yes Isobel, and you're not Jesus Christ!"

Thankfully, she laughed at my retort. I suggested she do some exercises with me to explore her beliefs about money and where they came from (those exercises are at the end of this chapter).

I then explained to her that many of our limiting beliefs about money come from our families, and therefore from our ancestors. We don't need to go too far back in history to understand why we may have these beliefs. Our DNA contains the history of our ancestors, so many of us hold imprints of poverty, hardship, starvation, slavery and low self-worth.

As late as the industrial revolution, many rich people WERE bad people, taking advantage of the poor for their own gain. They really were greedy and so the beliefs that it's greedy to be rich and rich people are bad are based on our ancestral history. Many religions encouraged sacrifice and poverty as a virtue, and people took vows of poverty when they entered a religious order. Sacrifice and charity were encouraged by most religious institutions, hence the belief that it wasn't spiritual to take money from anyone.

Women are more predisposed to these beliefs than men because for centuries married women could not own or inherit property. These laws did not end until 1862 in the United States and 1870 in the United Kingdom. Many of us are still energetically carrying these imprints of disempowerment when it comes to money. Most women were discouraged or even prevented from going into business. Even up to 40 years ago, middle-class women were not allowed to handle money, and having a job was seen as a sign of financial desperation.

By the time our session ended, Isobel's head was spinning.

"I've never realised just how much limitation there was within me around money! I really thought I had good ideals, but now I see it quite differently."

"Do you feel deserving of being rich?" I asked her.

"I'm starting to come round to the idea that I'm worthy of more than I'm allowing in right now."

"Who better than you to be making good money? You are

healing people. You are making a positive difference to people's lives. And I am sure you will put the money you make to good use and make the world a better place with it."

Affirmations

Money can create all that is good.

It is virtuous to be abundant.

It is spiritual to be rich.

It is wonderful to be rich.

I can contribute to a better world when I have money.

Pam's Story - It's wrong to focus on money, It's not OK to talk about money, If you focus on money you don't care about people

Pam was a meditation teacher who made very little money in her business and was thinking of shutting up shop and going back to her old job. I could see why she was in financial difficulty. She spoke about her business as if it were a cause or a charity. Rather than charging a set fee for her classes, Pam suggested that participants make a donation. The donations she received were small and certainly not creating enough income for Pam to live on. Because Pam felt awkward talking about money, she found it difficult to state a fee.

"Ideally, what would you like to be earning each month?" I asked her.

Pam looked uncomfortable. *"Well, more than I do now."*

I reflected back to Pam that she looked uncomfortable.

"Yes, I'm not OK talking about money. It doesn't seem right." Pam was about ten years older than me, so I understood that like me, she would have grown up in a family where it wasn't OK to talk about money.

I explained to Pam **The Universal Law of Giving and Receiving** and how the Universe worked through exchange. If there was not an effective exchange going on, her business was unlikely to flow. People who give too much attract people who take too much. Many women are great at giving but uncomfortable with receiving.

"Pam, do you believe that if you give more focus to making money, you are not caring about your clients?"

"Yes."

"That is just a belief. And that belief is attracting people who are happy to take but not exchange very much in return. When you believe in a fair exchange of energy, you will attract to you those who also believe in a fair exchange of energy."

Pam pondered this statement but didn't respond. I could see that she wasn't ready or willing to delve more deeply into her beliefs, so we left it at that.

Affirmations

It is divinely right to focus on purpose and money.

It is safe to talk about money.

I can focus on money and care about people.

Jamie's Story - It's ONLY money

Even though Jamie was a successful building contractor, he had little to show for it.

"I know I should have more to show for myself by now," said Jamie who had been making good money in his business for the last eight years, *"but I never seem to get ahead."*

"What do you spend your money on?" I asked him.

I gave Jamie pen and paper and asked him to list everything he spent his money on in the last month.

When we went through Jamie's list, it became clear that he wasn't valuing or respecting his money; in fact it appeared that he was doing all he could to get rid of it as fast as he could each month!

He told me about his childhood and how he grew up in a family of six children. His father had been a builder's labourer. On some weeks he made good money and other weeks he didn't. The family had no savings. They lived week-to-week. When there was money, they would spend it all and "live it up".

Life was either a feast or a famine. *"Oh well, it's only money,"* his mother would say. I suggested to Jamie that, like many people, he hadn't been shown how to manage money effectively or to treat it with respect. It wasn't his parents' fault; they would have been unconsciously doing what they had learned from their own families. Jamie let out a sigh of relief.

"Thank you! I feel like you've given me permission to think about me," Jamie said. He could see that this unconscious pattern was sabotaging his future happiness.

I got Jamie to think about what he wanted in the long-term and then create some financial goals. We then went about creating a simple plan so that he could achieve these goals.

Affirmations

I choose to respect and value the money I make.

I choose to use my money wisely.

I now no longer sabotage my wealth.

I stay true to my long term financial goals.

Manifesting income

What is your ideal business income? It's good to have a long-term goal and a short-term goal. Make your long-term goal as big as you wish, but make your short-term goal realistic for you to begin with.

This way you're far more likely to manifest it than if you make a goal that doesn't feel reachable. Then you build your manifesting muscle slowly but surely. As you begin to manifest what you know is achievable, you'll open up to higher possibilities incrementally. You cannot run before you can walk.

While it's wise to have an amount of money as a goal, don't get overly attached to that goal. Overlay that goal with another very simple intention - to manifest as much money as you need each month so as to live your best life.

"Money is only a tool. It will take you wherever you wish, but it will not replace you as the driver."

Ayn Rand

Crafting Your Spiritual Business Plan

Exercise 12 - Journaling

Tick or circle any of the self-limiting beliefs that feel like yours

- Nice people don't talk about money
- Money doesn't grow on trees (or there is never enough money)
- There is only ever so much to go around
- You have to work very hard to make money
- You cannot do work you love AND make good money
- It's wrong to take money from people
- Money is the root of all evil
- It is virtuous to be poor
- It's not good to be rich
- Rich people are bad people
- It's not spiritual to be rich
- It's greedy to be rich
- It's wrong to focus on money
- If you focus on money, you don't care about people
- It's ONLY money.

For every belief you have ticked, write down any key memories that come to mind where you were given this message (write about as many memories as you wish, but do not be concerned if you cannot think of any).

Refer back to the healing affirmations provided in this chapter for every self-limiting belief you have, and commit to saying these affirmations at the beginning and end of every day for the next six weeks. The affirmations are also in the back of this book.

Exercise 13 - Short Term and Long Term Financial Goals

Write down how much money ideally you would like to make per month NOW. Make this a BELIEVABLE amount.

Write down how much money ideally you would like to make per month IN FIVE YEARS TIME. Allow yourself to go beyond what you think is possible now.

Take a few minutes to visualise each of these two outcomes until you are in the feeling place of them. Give thanks to the Universe in advance.

Exercise 14 - A Prayer for Divine Abundance

Be still and allow yourself to feel quiet and calm.

Say the following prayer to the Universe:

I surrender to You my desire to be abundant.
I surrender to You all belief in lack and limitation.
I surrender to You my old self-limiting beliefs around money.
May I be filled with the truth that abundance is my Divine birthright.
I give gratitude in advance.
Thank You.

Chapter 6
Transform Your Relationship with Life

What you believe about life will either expand or limit your growth, success and happiness

Life is a big subject - it covers everything. In this chapter I want to share with you some key areas of life that can either hinder you and your business or enhance you and your business.

I have met with many people who find life a struggle, because they have a poor relationship with at least one of these areas of life:

- Time
- Surrender
- Gratitude
- Oneness
- Balance
- Courage

- Presence and Awareness
- Love.

Many of us hold limiting beliefs about these key areas of life that we may not even be aware of.

Time

How often have you thought or said the words *"I don't have enough time"?* Many of us live in a world where we feel a constant lack of time, attempting to jam into a day everything that we believe is required of us so as to live a happy and abundant life, and yet the lack of time sabotages our sense of happiness and abundance!

The four most common limiting beliefs we have about time are:

- There is never enough time
- Time is something we have to battle against
- Working hard is a good use of time
- Doing nothing or enjoying our leisure means wasting time.

And yet the truth is:

- There is always enough time for anything that is truly in your highest good
- When we love time and are grateful for it, it works with us

- When we work with love and inspiration, we are using our time well
- When we truly enjoy our time away from work, we are using our time well.

My realisations about time

Many years ago I remember feeling like there were never enough hours in a day. No matter how much I did, there was always more to be done. The list was never-ending. I was grumpy a lot of the time. And then one day at work I read a simple quote on a date calendar:

"You will never have enough time to do all the things you don't need to do."

Those words made an impact on me. *All the things you don't need to do!* It got me contemplating all the things that I was doing that I didn't need to be doing. It got me thinking about the essentials; the truly important things that I valued. It got me thinking about WHY I felt that certain things were so necessary when perhaps they really weren't and WHY I was doing them. It got me thinking about simplifying my life.

This made me aware that I had been doing things because I felt I should as opposed to doing them because I really wanted to do them. I became aware of how much I was doing just to please others, as opposed to pleasing myself. I also became aware of the need to be busy so as to assure myself that I was purposeful and successful.

Truth Number 1: Your time here is valuable. Use it for what is truly important to you.

Affirmation: *I always have enough time for what is truly important.*

Later on in my life I became aware of another truth about time. Time was not the set plane that most of us believe it to be. I began to see how time would speed up when I felt I had a lack of it, how it would slow down when I wasn't stressed or worried about the amount of time I had and that it would appear to stand still when I was fully absorbed in something I was doing.

When I chose to believe that I would have enough time for something, I would feel joyful and relaxed, and I would always be given the perfect amount of time.

Albert Einstein told us:

"When you sit with a nice girl for two hours, it seems like two minutes; when you sit on a hot stove for two minutes, it seems like two hours. That's relativity."

Truth Number 2: Time expands or contracts in accordance to how we are feeling.

Affirmation: *Time works with me and not against me.*

And only a few years ago, another truth about time showed itself to me. One morning three clients cancelled their appointments one after the other, which is highly unusual.

Then I received a phone call from one of my sons. It was an emergency and he needed me. The Universe was actually managing my time for me!

We will always be given enough time for that which is in our highest good; in fact the Universe will give it to us even if we haven't asked, if we just trust.

Rabindranath Tagore wrote:

"The butterfly counts not months but moments, and has time enough."

Already encoded within you is your soul mission and the time that it takes to achieve it, so there really is no point in worrying or stressing about time.

Truth Number 3: You will always have enough time to complete your soul's mission if you choose to live purposefully.

Affirmation: *The Universe gives me the perfect amount of time to achieve my soul mission.*

Never forget **The Universal Law of Timing**. Let go and allow the Universe's timing, which is always perfect. This leads me to our next key area of life.

Surrender

The problem for most people is that they do not surrender enough. In fact, the idea of surrender is foreign and frightening to many people, and may be seen as "giving up".

This couldn't be further from the truth. Surrendering is not giving up; it is handing over.

William Booth, founder of the Salvation Army said:

"The greatness of a man's power is the measure of his surrender."

The ego mind is the part of us that thinks it's all alone and has to manage everything, but our Higher Self knows that the Universe is the Supreme Intelligence which orchestrates all things.

Look at the seasons, the tides and the ways of nature. This is **The Universal Law of Rhythm.** There is a time for all things under Heaven if we just let go and allow. When you bring the concept of surrender into your daily life, miracles happen.

You can surrender your day and all that you wish to achieve, you can surrender your problems and challenges, your worries and your fears, your hopes and your dreams, knowing that this Divine Intelligence knows far better than you, how to go about it all and will manifest all manner of things in the best way possible.

Brendon's Story - The power of surrender

Brendon, the life coach who I introduced you to in Chapter 4, who was struggling to attract enough people to attend his first workshop, was certainly using **The Universal Law of Action**, but ignoring **The Universal Law of Surrender.** By surrendering the outcome, Brendon would be *co-creating*.

I asked Brendon to surrender his fear of failure and his ego mind's fearful thoughts of "not enough". I then asked him to visualise his workshop full of enthusiastic people until he was in the feeling place of it, and then *surrender* that vision to the Universe. Brendon smiled and looked peaceful.

Knowing that we have the support of this Great Intelligence, we can relax. As we come to see and know the miracles that can manifest from this Intelligence, we gain ever greater trust.

Truth Number 4: By surrendering, we allow the Supreme Intelligence to orchestrate.

Affirmation: *I surrender and let go, trusting in a Greater Intelligence than mine.*

Gratitude

Never underestimate the power of gratitude - the acknowledgement and appreciation for all that we have right now *and all that we will have in the future*, because the feelings of peace and love that gratitude brings, create the perfect vibration to draw more to you. This is **The Universal Law of Gratitude.**

By default, the ego mind will slip into fear and lack thinking, so a proactive practice of gratitude is essential to counteract this old conditioned thinking pattern.

Beginning and ending our day with a gratitude practice is the perfect way to stay in a high vibration of peace and love.

Brendon's Story - Giving gratitude in advance

I instructed Brendon to complete his visualising and surrendering process with giving thanks for the best possible outcome. As I shared in Chapter 4, Brendon manifested four attendees for his first workshop. I asked him to give thanks to the Universe every time someone signed up, as opposed to dropping into "lack" thinking which the ego mind will do (*"Is that all there is?"*). I explained to Brendon that unless we are grateful for all that we have now, we won't ever be grateful for what we receive in the future. Gratitude is the only vibration from which to grow one's dreams.

Brendon later reported that having four attendees at his first workshop worked well, as he didn't feel overwhelmed or stressed by too many people's needs. As Brendon's confidence and knowledge grew, his workshop attendances got larger too. He kept up the practice of gratitude and Brendon could see that the Universe was working perfectly for him from the start.

Truth Number 5: Gratitude creates the perfect vibration for all things to flourish.

Affirmation: *I give gratitude for all that I have and all that I shall have.*

Oneness

The ego views the world as dualistic:

- Them and us
- You and me

- This or that
- Up and down
- Left or right.

Beyond the world of the ego however, everything is one and we are all one. Hence **The Law of Karma (or cause and effect)** which deems that whatever we do to anyone, we do to ourselves, because you are your neighbour and your neighbour is you! Bad deeds will always come back to us. The Universe always keeps the score.

The Bible tells us:

"Do unto others as you would wish them to do unto you."

So if you wish to create good karma for your business, never speak ill of anyone or do anything to harm anyone, and hold good intent towards everyone.

Truth Number 6: Speak of others with love and do for others with love and the good will return to you.

Affirmation: *I choose loving words and actions towards everyone and my good returns to me.*

Let go of the old paradigm belief in competition. In Universal mind, there are enough clients for everyone, enough business for everyone and enough money for everyone. The concept of competition arises from the ego mind that believes in lack.

When you keep the focus on you and what your business is about, you will not scatter your energy and place it where it doesn't need to be. Other people's businesses are other people's businesses!

Pam's Story - I'll never succeed with all the competition out there

Let's revisit Pam, the meditation teacher who found it difficult to talk about money and charge money. Pam also limited her business because she still believed in the concept of competition.

I had asked Pam to look online to get an idea of what other people were charging for meditation classes. The results were interesting - some meditation teachers were charging thousands of dollars for meditation courses, while others charged a humble $10 or $20 per class.

"There are so many people out there doing what I'm trying to do. Sometimes I think I'm fooling myself that I could ever get ahead in this business."

Pam's posture slumped and hopelessness was written all over her face. Rather than using this exercise purely to research pricing, Pam had fallen into a low vibration because she was looking at others through the lens of comparison and competition.

I asked Pam to bring the focus back to her and what she felt she was here to do, and to breathe out and let go of that old idea that there's only so much business to go around.

"From my perspective, I can see that the world is your oyster," I said to Pam. *"The Universe is showing you that there are many and varied ways of teaching meditation and charging for your classes."*

I shared with Pam a saying I say a lot:

"Comparison is the thief of joy."

There is little use comparing ourselves or our business with others, because we are all unique. No two people are alike and no business is exactly like any other. We will draw to us clients who are a vibrational match to us. I told Pam that in my suburb there were several women practising similar healing modalities to me and I wished them all well. Rarely did I get a client who had been a client of any of the other healers in my area. I also shared with Pam that in the early days of my business, I was still thinking in terms of comparison and competition and I noticed that when I thought that way, my energy felt scattered and weak. What made me feel good, clear and strong was the work I did and the passion I felt for it, so I focused on that. Those feelings, I now realise, are what drew clients and money to me.

Truth Number 7: Keep the focus on you and your purpose, and all good will come to you.

Affirmation: *When I lovingly keep the focus on me and my purpose, all good comes to me.*

If we are thinking in terms of comparison and competition, we are likely to be feeling a most unpleasant emotion: envy.

Envy comes from the ego mind or the wounded self who believes that there is only so much to go around. It thinks *"If you have what I want, then I can't have it."* This is an incorrect thought. In Divine Mind, there is infinite abundance. Whatsmore, if someone is achieving something that you desire, he or she is simply there to show you that you can have it too. This person or business wouldn't be in your field otherwise. Knowing this, we can wish others well and be grateful that they are sending us a sign that it is possible for us too.

The toxic emotion of envy blocks your good from coming to you. Send love and gratitude to everyone who is successful and has what you want, and see the good that starts to come your way.

Fiona's Story - Bitterness and envy were blocking her success

Fiona was the owner of a fashion boutique. Years before, she went into a business partnership with her friend Jessica. After two years of running a successful boutique, Fiona's business partner Jess announced that she wanted to go out on her own. Jess had a wealthy husband who was going to fund her next venture. Over the years she had become highly successful, opening several stores, while Fiona's business "just got by" and never really grew. Fiona had felt betrayed and let down by her friend. As she spoke of the past, I could see that she had never come to terms with what had happened, and that she was still holding feelings of bitterness and envy towards her former friend and business partner. Even the mention of Jess's name made Fiona recoil.

I suggested to Fiona that people come into our lives for a reason, a season or a lifetime. Perhaps Jess came into her life to get her started in business, but she was never going to stick around. It was time to forgive Jess so that Fiona could free herself. I explained how the toxic emotions of resentment and envy were harming Fiona and her business, not Jess and her business. Fiona and I did a Soul Truth Healing process together and in this healing I asked Fiona to thank Jess for showing her what she could have too. Fiona felt an amazing shift after our session.

Truth Number 8: Those who have what you desire are there to show you that you can have it too.

Affirmation: *I release all envy and choose to be happy for those who have what I want.*

Balance

We live in a world of polarities:

- Left and right
- Yin and yang
- Hot and cold
- Work and play
- Rich and poor.

The Universal Law of Balance deems that balance is the key to everything. Nature is always seeking to balance itself and if we are to live our best lives, we must seek balance in all things too. Wherever our lives are out of balance, we will suffer.

Aaron's Story - Highly successful but exhausted

Aaron was a busy and successful hairdresser. He owned a salon and employed other talented stylists, but because he was so good at what he did, he was in constant demand. Work had begun to take over his whole life. He was becoming irritable towards his staff and even towards some of his clients. I suggested that he needed to create stronger boundaries around his personal life and to not allow work to encroach on personal time.

"I find it so hard to say no. I really don't want to let any of my clients down."

"What's the worst that can happen if you have to say no or suggest they see another stylist in the salon or book them in to see you in a few weeks?"

"They may go elsewhere and I'll lose the business."

So beneath Aaron's inability to create boundaries between his work life and his personal life was the fear that if he said "no", the business would dry up. I shared with Aaron that I had the same fear in the early days of my business too. However, when I began to create stronger boundaries between work and personal time, an interesting phenomenon took place. Most clients were more than happy to wait to see me, and the ones who wanted to go elsewhere were meant to go elsewhere. The Universe doesn't want us to sacrifice in order to be successful. The Universe wants us to enjoy a balance of work time and play time. When we get adequate rest and play, we get refreshed and this enhances our work.

And when we do good work, this enhances our leisure time.

I suggested that if Aaron continued to live an unbalanced life, he may manifest circumstances that force balance upon him - anything from upsetting more clients to having an accident because of tiredness or even an illness. Better to proactively embrace **The Universal Law of Balance** now than have it forced upon him in the future in a way that he had no control over.

Truth Number 9: Seek balance in all things.

Affirmation: *Balance is key to my true success.*

Courage

It takes courage to work for yourself, to be willing to grow and to change. Courageous people aren't fearless people. Courageous people acknowledge their fear and move through it so as to get to where they want to be. The writer Anais Nin wrote:

"Life shrinks or expands according to one's courage."

Having courage means being willing to go beyond your comfort zone, to keep challenging yourself and being willing to transform. It requires taking risks and facing failure from time to time, and being willing to try again. All of these things are necessary if you are in your own business and wanting to achieve true success.

Leah's Story - Moving through fear

You may recall Leah who had a fear of public speaking. By being willing to explore that fear and why she had it and to do some proactive healing work on it, Leah was able to speak to a large audience about her business. This not only was good for Leah's business and her online presence; she was able to give inspiration to other entrepreneurs. But Leah shared with me later that the real gift was knowing that she had the ability to transcend a limitation.

"If I can do that," said Leah. "What can't I do?"

Truth Number 10: Courage is the ability to move through fear to get to where you want to go.

Affirmation: *I have the courage to move beyond old limitations and to grow.*

Presence and Awareness

Transformation is not possible without some degree of presence and awareness. Presence is the ability to be in the present moment fully. Presence cultivates awareness. Awareness is the ability to observe - your surroundings, what's going on in those surroundings, and yourself and what is going on within yourself. Of course we are not always going to be fully present and fully aware because our mind gets caught up in thoughts constantly.

As suggested earlier in this book, regularly practising meditation and/or quiet contemplative time are essential to cultivating presence and awareness. There is a simple meditation practice provided in the back of this book. When you are present and aware, you have the ability to gauge your own vibration, and you can ask yourself:

- Am I at peace with time?
- Am I feeling surrendered?
- Am I feeling grateful?
- Am I at one with everyone and everything?
- Am I feeling balanced?
- Am I feeling courageous?
- Am I present in the here and now?

The more present and aware we are, we have the ability to respond to people and situations mindfully, as opposed to reacting in old ineffective ways. Responding as opposed to reacting is key to every aspect of your business.

Truth Number 11: Presence and awareness are essential for transformation.

Affirmation: *In presence and awareness. I respond mindfully.*

Love

What is love? Love is the highest and most pure vibration there is, and the key to achieving success. Being mindful of being a loving presence in all that we do ensures we not only manifest our desires, but we do so in the most enjoyable way and we create good karma as well.

The Universal Law of Karma deems that we reap what we sow. The love for ourselves and our purpose is essential on this journey.

Loving all those we come into contact with - our clients, our employees and contractors, our advisors and helpers - allows everything to flow. The old saying *"Love makes the world go around"* really is true. Wherever we are devoid of love, we will experience blockages and difficulties.

In essence, we are all love. Become aware of your heart and see and feel yourself each day as a loving presence. Even though we may experience difficult people and relationships, it is wise to go within and take responsibility for your part in any relationship by asking yourself

"What is it in me that is stopping me from loving this person?"

Be willing to love everyone. This doesn't mean that you don't have personal boundaries; it simply means to be kind and to hold good will towards everyone.

Truth Number 12: Love creates all good things.

Affirmation: *I am a loving presence always.*

"The greatest glory in living lies not in failing, but in rising every time we fail."

Nelson Mandela

Crafting Your Spiritual Business Plan

Exercise 15 - Journaling

Rate between 1 and 10 (1 being very low and 10 being very high) your relationship with each key area of life below:

- Time
- Surrender
- Gratitude
- Oneness
- Balance
- Courage
- Presence and Awareness
- Love

How could you improve each of these areas?

- Time
- Surrender
- Gratitude
- Oneness
- Balance

- Courage
- Presence and Awareness
- Love

Exercise 16 - A Prayer of Intention

Be still and allow yourself to feel quiet and calm.

Say the following prayer to the Universe:

Today may I be at peace with time.
May I surrender to Your grace.
May I be grateful and appreciative for all that I have.
May I be at one with everyone and everything.
May I enjoy balance.
May I be courageous.
May I be present and aware.
May I be love.

Chapter 7
Soulfully Successful Marketing

Getting yourself and your business out there is necessary if you are to expand and grow your business.

The purpose of this chapter is to encourage you to get comfortable with putting you and your services or products out into the world and to find a way that works for you, because the most important thing when it comes to marketing, is to feel joyful, peaceful and inspired by the process, not fearful, hopeless or pessimistic. Remember that you are your business and your business is you. How you feel really does affect the results of any marketing effort.

Marketing your business is an essential part of growing your business, yet it also brings up a lot of fear and resistance for many people. There are myriad ways of marketing, and what works for somebody else's business may not work for yours and vice versa. Every business is unique and will require its own unique marketing strategy.

There are plenty of books, online courses and social media marketing specialists available to entrepreneurs when it comes to strategy, but at the end of the day, it is important to follow your own gut instinct as well. I am proposing a soulful approach to marketing, away from the hard-selling and manipulation that is currently offered by some marketing "experts".

Here are some key points when it comes to marketing:

- Accept that putting your business "out there" is essential to growing your business
- Be willing to invest in your business
- Acknowledge any fear you have of putting yourself or your business "out there"
- Consider all your options (and there are many options!)
- Spend what you can afford on marketing
- Be detached but also track your outcomes
- Understand that most successful marketing emerges out of trial and error.

Putting yourself "out there"

Marketing is an essential aspect of being in business, and yet it is also one which brings up a lot of fear and timidity for many people. Most of us think of marketing and advertising as something that is "pushy", that endeavours to get people's attention by taking their attention away from something else; that we are in some way tricking people or enforcing our will upon them. Many of us see marketers and advertisers as selfish tricksters. This is very much an old paradigm egoic view of marketing and advertising.

If you really think about it, all that marketing is, is letting people know that you, your services or your products exist. You, your services or your products are here ready and willing to help in the way they do, and those who need and like you, your products or your services may be willing to exchange money for what you have to offer, because they need what you are offering. As I write this, I am reminded of the Louise Hay affirmation:

"That which I seek is also seeking me."

Louise Hay was also the author of the affirmation:

"People are in need of my services."

These affirmations remind us that we, our services or our products are wanted and needed. If you have a need or a desire to fulfill a purpose, you can be sure that there will be people in need of what you have to offer.

The ego mind that believes in lack and limitation will have us believe that this is not the case, and that it's going to be a fight, a battle or a struggle to get noticed in the marketplace. At the other end of the spectrum, some people have unrealistic expectations and believe that their marketing efforts will be an overnight success. The truth usually lies somewhere in the middle (The Universal Law of Balance).

Acknowledge the fear

It's not uncommon to feel paralysing fear if you're about to market yourself, your products or your services for the very first time. Underlying this fear can be:

- Fear of judgment
- Fear of failure
- Fear of humiliation
- Fear of success and the unknown.

Jane's Story - This is terrifying!

Jane was about to launch her business and her new website. She was very pleased with the way it looked, but she couldn't bring herself to press the button to make her website go "live".

"I'm terrified of putting myself out there," she said.

I asked Jane if she felt that by putting herself out there, something terrible might happen.

"Yes. It feels like that, even though it doesn't make any sense."

I could relate to what Jane was going through. I had been through the same fear myself and later on when I was creating online courses and I began my social media marketing, I felt the same terror again. And I don't use the word "terror" lightly. Beneath the fear of putting ourselves out there are not just the fears we hold from this life, but the fears that we hold in our DNA from our ancestors and even our past lives. This terror is particularly strong for women. Empowered women really did experience some terrible things throughout history, and for many of us it's still sitting there in our DNA, even though we live in far friendlier times.

Jane appeared more relaxed after I explained this to her. Just acknowledging fear and knowing there is always a good reason why we have it is healing in itself, because on top of her fear, Jane was going into self-judgment and shame. She could now let that go, with a greater understanding of what was really going on.

Impostor Syndrome

It's very common to experience "impostor syndrome" when you first decide to market yourself, your products or your services. The fear of judgment in the form of:

- "Who does she think she is?"
- "They call themselves an expert?"
- "She's making a complete fool of herself"
- "She's bound to fail!"

These are just a reflection of the judgments we have of ourselves and that old belief that we're not good enough.

My Story - The judgments were a mirror of my fears

Not that long ago it became apparent through both inner and outer guidance that my work was to become more global. I had achieved success at a local level - I had plenty of clients as a healer and coach and my workshops and meditation evenings were well-attended. As if by magic, Ben came back into my life. We had worked together before, recording meditations for the Insight Timer app, and I was thrilled that this creative and spiritual soul was now free to work for me three days a week. Producing my online courses, publishing and marketing were to be Ben's domain.

Ben encouraged me to start producing content for social media marketing. As we put it "out there" into the ether, I was met with both positive and negative reactions from those around me, but mostly *negative*. As I experienced these reactions, I observed the fear, self-judgment and shame that came up within me. I then realised that each person who made negative comments was just a mirror of my own lack of belief in myself and my fear of judgment. Knowing this, I could then silently thank the person for showing me something I needed to work on in myself. As I worked on each aspect, the judgments and negative comments from others fell away. They no longer needed to do me the favour of holding up the mirror!

Courage

If you recall in our last chapter, I wrote about courage. Courage isn't being fearless; it's acknowledging your fear and being willing to move through it. A very interesting thing happens when we choose to face a fearful situation and dive right into it. The fear dissolves, and what we feared no longer has any power over us. The metaphysicist Florence Scovell-Schin wrote:

"If one is willing to do a thing he is afraid to do, he does not have to face a situation fearlessly; and there is no situation to face; it falls away of its own weight."

Marketing in the Age of Creativity

Marketing and promotion is a "sum of its parts" kind of game, and it will have a cumulative impact. There is no one strategy or formula or promotional tool to invest in to get the secret answers of marketing, because we are living in a time where our marketing options are many and varied; in fact there is so much choice that it can be confusing and daunting. The world and technology are changing so fast that new options and new marketing fads are appearing all the time.

If you recall my story back in Chapter 2, I was approached by an internet deal company to run a Reiki deal. Those online deal companies were extremely popular back in 2011, but now we barely hear of them. The Universe offered me a particular marketing opportunity that was happening back then, and I happily rode that wave.

In 2017 I was introduced to a free meditation app and it occurred to me to record the meditations I had written for my meditation evenings over the years, as it would be a great way to get my content out there and to help others. I didn't do it for the money; there was no money to be had from the app back then. My meditations became quite popular.

Within a year of uploading my meditations, Insight Timer announced that they wanted to pay their teachers. I was now earning a passive income from something I didn't even realise I could make money from!

Later on in this chapter, I will be sharing with you some marketing ideas, but please be aware that even as this book goes into print, change is happening faster and faster, and so mindful awareness is essential if we are to embrace the right opportunities as they appear.

The Financial Aspect of Marketing

Any way you look at it, marketing is going to cost you, be it in time, energy or money. Never resent the time, energy or money that you spend on marketing, as it is an essential cost of being in business. Resentment will block your good from coming to you. Pay for your marketing costs with joy and the money will ultimately return to you, even if it's not from this particular round of marketing. Remember **The Universal Law of Action** - the Universe takes you seriously when you take action towards what you want, and will step in and support you.

Belinda's Story - Unwilling to invest in her herself and her business

Belinda was passionate about organic skincare and had created her own range of products, which were loved by her friends and family. She had drawn to her a small network of fans whom she sold to, but in order to make a decent living and for the production of these products to be viable, Belinda would have to go bigger than her immediate vicinity. This was currently more of a hobby than a business. Belinda would have to spend some money on marketing if she were to expand. She had begun posting on social media, but not boosting the posts as paid ads.

"If you want to make some money, you've got to spend some money," I told Belinda.

Belinda looked uncomfortable. *"It's going to cost me thousands of dollars to pay for a social media strategy,"* she said.

"Yes but it could be money well spent if it gets your products out there to a much wider audience. Do you have the funds to do this?"

"Yes," she replied, *"but I'm very aware I could lose that money."*

"Where is that money now?" I asked.

"I've invested it in shares."

"You could lose that money in shares too. You've got to work out whether you think YOU are worth investing in, or if you trust the stock market more than your own heart and soul that created something that you believe to be of true value."

I realised my statement was confronting, but I had asked myself the same confronting question only a year before.

Why was I willing to invest in certain corporations but not in what I'm here to do?

Answer: *You don't believe you're worth investing in!* And if YOU don't believe you're worth investing in, why would anybody else think you're worth investing in? It's got to start with you!

Your marketing budget

When it comes to working out how much to spend on marketing, I give the same stock-standard answer to everyone. Spend what you can afford, and by "afford" I mean an amount that is not going to put you into the vibration of fear and lack. By all means, sacrifice a few "pleasures" for your marketing budget, but do not sacrifice essentials, and do not put yourself in debt because this will take you into a place of fear and lack immediately, and have you desperately clinging to a positive outcome.

Harry's story - Overinvesting in marketing

Harry had done a remarkable job of moving forward with his new business after his sabbatical in South America a year before. He had come to see me again, and looked despondent. He had invested $15,000 on a six month online coaching class to master the marketing of his business, and the strategies he had learned were not working for him.

"Gosh Harry, that's a lot of money," I said as I clicked over in my head how many helpful and dynamic sessions he could have had with me for that money, and been well on his way.

"When I saw this course, it promised me everything I needed to know, so I thought it a worthwhile investment." Harry shared with me that he had exorbitant credit card debt now, and felt even more desperate than ever for his business to work out.

I shared with Harry that years ago a very important truth dropped into my psyche - that whatever was in my highest good would be easily affordable and easily do-able at the time. Anything that was too difficult in any way, including financial, was not meant for me. When I embraced this concept, I became clear on what was for me and what wasn't for me.

"That's so true." said Harry. *"I feel like even more of a failure now than ever, because the online coach is telling me that I 'should' be attracting more business to me by now."*

"We are all unique Harry and our businesses are unique. Comparison is the thief of joy. Ok, so tell me what you did get out of this course. Everything has something to teach us."

Harry told me a few things that had helped him, but he realised the most important lesson: Anything that is too difficult in any way - including financial - was not meant for him.

"This is great Harry. You've learned a really important lesson, and when you embrace a lesson, forgiving yourself and everyone involved, the Universe sends you Divine Compensation."

I got Harry to recite a Prayer of Divine Compensation:

"I realise that I made a choice not in my highest good.
I embrace the lesson from this experience.
I forgive myself and all involved.
Thank You for now sending to me my Divine compensation."

I received a call from Harry two days later. He had received a cheque from the Tax Office for $10,000. **The Universal Law of Divine Compensation** was already onto it. I have every faith that the Universe will make up the other $5,000 in another miraculous way for Harry in Divine and perfect timing. I could share with you many similar stories of Divine compensation including my own, but I think Harry's story illustrates the point perfectly.

Let Go of Outcomes

No matter how you choose to market yourself, your products or your services, let go of outcomes. This is **The Universal Law of Detachment.** It's our attachment to an outcome that leads to us judging ourselves as a failure or a success.

In his poem *"If"*, Rudyard Kipling writes:

> *"If you can meet with triumph and disaster,*
> *And treat those two impostors just the same."*

The ego fixates on immediate outcomes, but it is the *long term* outcomes that really matter. If a marketing effort doesn't achieve the outcome you wanted, do not give up. Very often, a snowballing effect takes place - over time you will build:

- More followers (if you are marketing through social media)
- More good reviews
- More business

- More clients
- More profit
- More knowledge
- More expertise.

It is the ego that wants immediacy. It is the ego that wants instant results. It is the ego that will have you believe you are a failure if you haven't gotten the outcome you hoped for.

Track your outcomes - what works and what doesn't

Notice what works and what doesn't. This may sound contradictory to letting go of outcomes, but it really isn't. Let go of any ATTACHMENT to outcomes, but at the same time, track the outcomes. When you get a good response from a particular marketing strategy, do it some more. When you don't get a good response, let that strategy go.

Focus on giving and not getting

When you choose to market yourself, your services or your products, do not make money and profit your primary focus. Make your purpose and the *Why?* your primary focus. When you think and feel in terms of giving and not gaining, you are working in alignment with the Universe. When you choose to give away something valuable, the good will return to you. Content that is helpful and valuable to people will draw more business to you ultimately, because people will begin to trust you. Giving away free samples is also a great idea. As I wrote earlier, my uploading of free meditations on Insight Timer came from a place of wanting to share something I knew to be of value. My meditation groups loved the guided meditations I wrote, so why not share them on an app where they could be available to all?

It's important to note, however, that if you are choosing to give anything away, be sure you are doing this from a place of high self-worth and not low self-worth.

From a place of high self-worth, we are believing:

What I have to give is worthy and so I share it with love, knowing my good will return to me eventually.

From a place of low self-worth, we are believing:

Nobody wants what I have to give so I may as well give it away for free.

These are two very different vibrations and will create two extremely different outcomes.

To embrace the **Universal Law of Giving and Receiving**, consider what you are willing and able to give people which is of high value but still retains something for them to purchase if they resonate with you or your products. This could be anything, such as:

- A free small sample of your product
- An e-book
- A free short session
- A free video tutorial
- A discount coupon.

Your unique selling proposition

What is your unique selling proposition? What makes you or your product or your service different to everyone else out there? It is important to ponder this question, not only for your potential clients but also for yourself. When you get clear on what it is you are offering that is unique, you become more confident in what it is you are offering.

The power of authenticity

Do not force yourself to create a story because you think it will sell. Share yourself, services and products in a genuine, authentic way. People respond to authenticity.

Deliver what you promise

In any marketing campaign, be specific and clear with what you are offering and be sure to deliver. If you recall, I wrote earlier in Chapter 5:

"Money flows to those who can fix other people's problems."

So it is wise to consider:

- What problem am I solving?
- What solution am I offering?

Keep it current

Marketing messages that are relevant to what is going on in the "now" are going to appeal to many people. Marketing your products or services in relation to the "now" will have more immediacy.

Identifying your market

As much as you can, identify who is most likely to buy your goods or services, because this will make your marketing a lot easier. At first you may not know, but in time you will be shown by those who are doing business with you. This is another good reason to track your sales.

Existing clients are your greatest asset

Just like the old saying *"A bird in the hand is worth two in the bush"*, existing clients are more valuable than potential new clients. Why? Because they already know you or your product and will be invested in you to a greater degree than someone who doesn't know you and your products as yet. Existing clients may continue to buy from you as well as refer their friends and family to you. So as much as you can, give added value to your existing clients - special offers, gifts and extras.

The 4 main types of clients

While I am not a fan of categorising people in terms of their spending habits and expectations, the following information is helpful when it comes to marketing your business and drawing the right clients to you. Marketing researchers have identified that there are four main types of clients:

- **Irrationally free** – high maintenance, demanding and looking at how to get the same results for free if they weren't using you.

- **Price shoppers** – these people want a good deal and

may haggle with you.

- **Value seekers** – want good results at a fair price and they value what you do.
- **Premium buyers** – have more money than time, are focused on results and if they're getting results from you, they can be loyal, highly lucrative but also highly demanding.

Ideally, you want the majority of your clientele to be **value seekers**, followed by **premium buyers**. If you want to avoid the first two, do not market yourself as low-price.

In my personal experience, I have most enjoyed working with value seekers. These people believe in a fair exchange of energy, reflecting back my own belief in **The Universal Law of Balance** and the **Universal Law of Giving and Receiving**.

Outsourcing your marketing

Many people choose to outsource their marketing by employing a marketing strategist or a social media marketing manager, or educating themselves through marketing courses and seminars. Beware the lesson of Harry's story. You can easily spend money you cannot afford on marketing strategies that may not work for you or your product.

If considering outsourcing your marketing, it is wise to ask yourself:

- Can I afford to do this?
- Am I being sold false promises?

- Am I putting too much money, time or energy into this?
- What does my gut instinct tell me?

Marketing suggestions

There are a myriad of ways to market yourself and your business, so it is easy to feel overwhelmed when looking at all the options. Just because there are a lot of options however doesn't mean you have to embrace them all! In fact I would discourage this entirely. Starting off with what feels do-able and inspiring is a great way to start. Start with just one type of marketing, and remember that it really is a series of trial and error. Do not take on too much too soon.

Below is a list of marketing suggestions that are relevant at this time.

Website

Without a doubt, a website is not only a marketing tool, it is essential for any business. The first thing most people do when they hear about a product or service they want is to search for it online.

A website can contain as much or as little as you wish to share about your product or service. It is the perfect space for a potential client/customer to learn more about you and your service or product. In addition, any other marketing material will refer people to your website, be it flyers, online ads, business cards or social media.

Business cards

Business cards are still used by many people and are a great way to softly market your goods and services. To use business cards effectively, keep them on you at all times!

Mailing list

This is a most effective marketing tool because *the clients you already have are more valuable than potential new clients.* Ensure when you meet a new client or receive email enquiries, that you get their email address. By law you need to ask for their permission to go on your mailing list. With a mailing list, you can send out newsletters, updates and special offers. Many clients forward on your mail-outs to friends and family if what you have to say or offer is of value.

Social Media

Facebook / Instagram / LinkedIn / Twitter - also a highly effective way of marketing if you have the knowledge on how to do this effectively yourself or if you outsource to a professional.

Create a business page on any of these social media platforms. Ask your clients to like your page. Posts can be seen by your followers, but also promoted to specific audiences. To advertise effectively through social media, I advise more specific reading, research and planning before beginning your marketing campaign.

YouTube

You can create your own YouTube channel and create a YouTube video or a series of videos that are either entertaining or helpful and demonstrate your product or expertise in your field. You can also pay to advertise on YouTube, however I would advise adequate research and planning prior to using this form of marketing.

Free talks, demonstrations or events

You can create these to go online or you can hold them in a physical space for attendees to showcase your goods or services.

Trade shows and festivals

Displaying your products or services in a relevant space to your business can be very effective.

Flyers

This is a good strategy for many businesses, because flyers can be printed reasonably cheaply and it costs nothing to have them displayed in places such as local notice boards, cafes and any other business willing to support you. Choose places that draw the right demographic in your local area.

Google Ads

Google ads can be expensive but effective if you know how to implement them, and they may place your website in a higher ranking in searches.

Traditional Advertising

Advertising in newspapers, magazines, television, radio - This type of advertising can be very expensive but suitable and profitable for certain types of businesses.

Blog

Writing a blog that is helpful to your potential customers and clients will (a) help them and (b) allow them to get to know you and your services. This can also assist with building your website's search engine reach.

Think of creating topical blog posts that go to the heart of what your prospective clients need.

Joint ventures

Teaming up with others in their own business can create some great products/services with amazing results where you each get to benefit from the other's client base.

Podcast

Being interviewed on a podcast can be a wonderful way to promote your services and also share good content. Creating your own podcast is also a good option if you have the time, energy and inspiration to do so.

Write a book

Writing a book that backs up the work you do can be an effective marketing tool, as it is (a) helpful to the right people, (b) creates a relationship between you and the reader and (c) showcases your expertise.

You can publish your book in physical form, as an e-book or as an audio-book, or all three!

Free e-book

Write an e-book that is helpful and make it available on your website, e-book platforms or in your ad campaigns. Be sure that the content is relevant and valuable. This is a great way of offering people something of value in exchange for their email address, thus building your mailing list.

Business networking groups

There are business networking groups in many towns and cities, and in each chapter, there is only one person in any given category of business. For example, there will be only one lawyer, one carpet salesman, one reiki healer. Business people come together to help each other and promote each other's businesses. These also exist online.

Word of mouth

Never underestimate the power of word of mouth. Personal referrals from one person to another will always be an effective and organic method of marketing. If what you are doing or selling is giving people positive results, you can be sure that word of mouth referrals will start happening.

The intuitive path is the way

It is wise to research all your marketing options, but pay attention to your gut instincts and hunches, for they are the messages from your intuitive self. By being present and aware, you will be able to see opportunities and seize them at the right time. Life is always handing us opportunities - in fact life offers us one opportunity after another, so do not be concerned if you have missed opportunities in the past.

The Universe is very good at offering second chances and even third chances. It is never too late to become present and embrace all the riches that life has to offer.

No matter what you do, do it with love

This is the most important aspect of marketing. If you market yourself, your services or your products with love and joy, you are in the correct vibration from which you will manifest. If you feel uneasy, resentful, fearful, resistant, uninspired or any other unloving emotion, it is likely that your marketing efforts will not grow your business. Love is the fertile soil through which your dreams will grow.

Get the Universe on board

Remember you are never alone. When you endeavour to market your business, surrender all that you do to the Divine Source, and ask to be shown the way. The Universe does not wish this to be hard for you. If anything feels too difficult or just not right, it is not the way!

A good product eventually sells itself

Effort is required at the beginning, but a good product eventually sells itself. Your marketing efforts create a snowballing effect. Over time, the momentum builds, the energy intensifies and your business will take on a life of its own. This is the Universal Flow!

"People tend to overestimate what they can do in the short term, and underestimate what they can do in the long term."

Bill Gates

Crafting Your Spiritual Business Plan

Exercise 17 - Journaling

Contemplate any fears you may have about marketing and putting yourself or your products out there. You can use the list below to identify your fears

- Fear of judgment
- Fear of failure
- Fear of humiliation
- Fear of success and the unknown.

What can you currently afford for your marketing budget?

What is your unique selling proposition?

To the best of your knowledge, who are the people most likely to buy your product or service?

Who are your ideal clients / customers?

How can you give added value to your existing clients?

What marketing ideas currently appeal to you?

Exercise 18 - A prayer for marketing your business

Be still and allow yourself to feel quiet and calm.

Say the following prayer to the Universe:

I surrender to You my marketing ideas.
Thank You for helping me every step of the way.
Thank you for Divine guidance and inspiration.
Thank You for showing me what is Divinely right and what is not.
May my business be taken to its highest potential
As a blessing on all the world.
Thank You.

Chapter 8
Your Ideal Work Day

Even though you have a vision for the future, your power rests in the Now. This power comes from being in a high vibration in the present moment and finding joy in each and every day, whatever the circumstances.

What would your ideal working day look like? Sometimes we can get so caught up with our future vision and achieving it, that we forget that the most important moment is the present one, and that each and every day is a gift in and of itself no matter where we are on our journey to success. As I said much earlier on in this book, it is the journey and not the destination that really counts, because the more you are enjoying the journey, the more likely you are to manifest the destination!

In this final chapter, I would like to share with you the importance of creating a daily structure and daily rituals to keep yourself in a high vibration. But let me first share with you a realisation I made quite a few years ago.

My realisation about daily struggle

I had just completed my NLP Master certification and I was full of inspiration and drive to apply the principles of NLP to myself and my business, and to create an effective way to share these practices with my clients. The problem was that I was SO full of inspiration and drive that I became overwhelmed by everything that I needed to do and to implement in order to achieve my goal. I became stressed and anxious and found myself back in my old pattern of "so much to do and not enough time". After at least a week of stressful hard work, my awareness kicked in. I got back on my meditation mat, and during the meditation a very clear message emerged.

If the path you are on feels like a continual uphill path of hardship and struggle, then it is not the way.

Instantly, I felt relief, before another message dropped in.

The path to your success will flow with grace and ease.

These messages filled me with joy and they also changed my perception of work entirely and the way I viewed each working day. I had been treating each day as an opportunity to get as much done as I could, regardless of how I felt. Now I could see that I was an important part of my day; not just my projects. I really began to understand the importance of:

- Self care
- Balance

- Discernment
- Spiritual connection
- Gratitude
- Intuition.

Let me expand on each point a little further.

Self care

You are the most important person in your life! Without you, your purpose and your business wouldn't exist. It is so easy to forget about yourself at times. Your wellbeing is of paramount importance. Most of us have been taught to sacrifice our needs for other people and other things, but in order to live our best lives, looking after ourselves on a daily basis must come first.

Balance

Learning to balance our personal needs with the needs of our business, our relationships and other commitments, as well as a balance of action and inaction are also important if we are to enjoy our daily lives. Some people fool themselves that they will finally re-balance when the project is over, when the weekend arrives or when they finally get to go on that holiday. When you bring balance into your daily life, you no longer yearn for a holiday!

Discernment

We cannot achieve balance and find the joyful path without discernment. We live in an age where we are constantly bombarded with outside messages and demands and a culture that values "busy-ness" over balance. Being able to discern what is important and what is not ensures that we do ENOUGH each day, but not too much. Discernment clears a space so that we are fully engaged and focused on the important tasks and the rituals that matter to us. Learning to say *"No"* without feeling guilty is one of the arts of discernment.

Spiritual connection

You are not taking this journey alone! When you bring daily spiritual practices into your life, you come to know on a daily basis that you've got company, and it is indeed very powerful company! You come to know at a core level that you are co-creating, and in this knowledge, you feel supported, and your work flows with grace and ease.

Gratitude

Practising gratitude each and every day creates a powerful vibration that gets you focussing on what you DO have and not on what you DON'T have. Gratitude literally changes your chemistry. To truly feel the benefits of gratitude, a daily practice is necessary. You can download a free gratitude journal from my website.

Intuition

The more you go within, the more you awaken your intuition. The intuitive path is the way to your dreams. When you have access to your own intuition, you will begin to work more intuitively, as opposed to working in a concretised way.

You will go more with your gut instincts, be more flexible and more open to listening to yourself and noticing outside signs and guidance.

Creating a daily structure

Caring for yourself and working intuitively doesn't mean that you don't have structure in your day. Working for yourself requires that you have at least some structure. Working without structure often leads to a lack of motivation and an inability to get real traction. While every day may be different, I would recommend that a basic working day structure would include:

- A morning ritual of self-care
- Work hours
- Meal times
- An end of day ritual and/or a bedtime ritual.

Being flexible

You can have a daily structure AND be flexible. If you are working intuitively, you allow yourself to be flexible within the structure.

For example, after your morning routine, you may have planned on working on a particular project, but it becomes apparent that something is more urgent or necessary that day, and so you choose to do that instead. Or it may be that an unexpected opportunity comes in that would be good for you or your business, and so you put your initial project on hold until tomorrow.

Let go of age of productivity thinking

The age of productivity - whereby the more you work, the more you produce and the more money you make - is over! It is no longer working for mankind. In this new age of creativity, it's not about working harder; it's about working smarter.

When we are truly present, connected to Source and aware, we have the ability to focus our attention fully on what we are doing. We intuitively know what to do, how much to do and when to stop. The Universe does not want us to work HARD and sacrifice our health or inner peace.

Beware of workaholism

For some people, work is a very real addiction, even if they are choosing to work for themselves. As children, they may have gotten the message that they were only worthwhile when they were achieving. Now, as adults, when they aren't achieving (or being "productive"), the workaholic feels like they are "nothing".

There are going to be times in our lives when we aren't achieving, or when we may be unable to work. Loving ourselves whether or not we are achieving is unconditional self-love, and the perfect state to be in if we are to achieve soulful success.

My routines and rituals

I'd like to share with you the routines and rituals that I have been doing for quite a few years now. I will also be providing these as exercises in your Spiritual Business Plan at the end of this chapter.

These rituals are naturally woven into my day and don't feel difficult or forced. Everyone needs to find a way that works for them. We are all different and have unique needs, so please do not think that I am prescribing for you what you need to do. Rather, I invite you to take and utilise what resonates with you, and let go of the rest!

My usual work day structure

My morning begins with getting up at the same time each day and doing 20 minutes of meditation as well as some Reiki on myself. I follow this with a prayer of intention and then surrender the day to the Universe, knowing that even though I have plans, the Universe is ultimately in charge of how my day would be best spent.

I am very fortunate to live in a beautiful harbourside suburb of Sydney, so my morning exercise will usually be a walk on Balmoral beach, followed by some yoga and then a swim. During my swim, I do my gratitude practice and say prayers.

I begin seeing clients mid-morning and take a break for lunch mid-afternoon.

My work involves not only seeing clients face-to-face, but holding workshops, hosting online events, writing books and meditations, recording meditations, creating marketing campaigns and giving interviews, so while I do plan ahead each week, flexibility within my working day is also important.

One day a week I have a client-free day where I attend to projects such as writing, planning, meeting with my assistant Ben and attending to admin tasks.

Although I see clients on Saturdays, I re-balance with a day off during the week to socialise, catch up on personal matters, go shopping or have a massage.

At the end of each day, I say an energy clearing prayer, to cleanse me of any negative energies I may have taken on during the course of the day, and then I give gratitude for all that I have achieved that day by giving myself a *"pat on the back"*. I then thank the Universe, for the privilege of doing the work that I love, for all my wonderful clients and my abundance.

Before going to sleep, I give gratitude again for the day and I call upon the Archangels to take me to the highest realms of love and light for my growth, evolution and enlightenment.

My Monday morning ritual

For quite a few years now, I have begun the week with a Monday morning ritual. This could also be done on a Sunday, as an early preparation for the week ahead. After a meditation, I put my "order" in with the Universe, stating my intentions and all that I would like to achieve and manifest for the week. I then surrender those intentions, knowing that if these requests are not realised, the Universe has other plans for me, which of course will be in my highest good.

During this process, I also surrender all my worries and challenges to the Universe. As I am also a reader of the tarot, I meditate on the challenges and then ask for guidance through the cards. I am always amazed at the answers that present themselves. I suggest that even if you do not read the tarot, buy a set of oracle cards that appeal to you, and use the cards in this way. This strengthens your connection to Source, and allows you to receive direct help.

When business is slow

There will be times when business is slow, particularly in the early days of a business. In these quiet times, you want to feel as peaceful as possible, and have absolute faith that the tide will turn and come back in. In the early days of my business, I would panic when business was quiet and feel the need to somehow "drum up" business, but this action-oriented solution didn't work for me. What I needed was a vibrational shift. By practising acceptance and seeing the quieter times as an opportunity rather than a disaster, my inner peace was restored, and when the time was right, business would flow right back in!

A charming old man who owned a local menswear store in my suburb shared with me what he did when business went quiet. He would close the shop for a few hours and go to a local cafe and have coffee! He chose to enjoy the gift of this quiet time. And always business would boom again. My client Sarah told me that when business was quiet she would go for a massage and allow herself to relax deeply. The phone would start ringing with new business straight after!

Quiet times are NOT the Universe telling you that you're a failure or that you should give up; it is the Universe giving you some time to replenish and refresh before the next wave of opportunity comes in. So if business is quiet, make the most of it and nurture yourself - do something you love and keep giving gratitude. Do anything that gives you a sense of inner peace and joy.

When business is too busy

Just as we need to feel peaceful when business is slow, we also need to find peace when business becomes too busy! Remember, the Universe doesn't want you to work HARD. If you find yourself too busy, surrender the situation to the Universe and reflect on what lesson you are meant to be learning. Is it:

- To allow more time and space by adjusting your time expectations
- To not overcommit or over-book yourself
- To say no
- To delegate
- To expand by getting a new contractor or employee.

Always, the answers lie within you. So even if you are overly busy, make the time to meditate and go within and find the answer. Trying to fix being overly busy by making yourself busier doesn't work - it just perpetuates the problem.

Work relationships

No matter what business you are in, business is all about relationships - your relationship with your customers or clients, your employees and contractors and any other people with whom you come into contact with in the course of your day. Be mindful every day of your relationships. The old saying "the customer is always right" is good advice, but I'd like to improve on that statement.

I believe that the customer is always:

- Worthy of respect
- Worthy of kindness
- Worthy of receiving good value.

And so are your employees and contractors and anyone else you come into contact with. The Golden Rule of treating others as you would like to be treated is paramount in creating good karma for yourself and your business.

There were times early on in my business, where I got overly focused on the project or the work at hand, and I would then lose sight of the importance of the relationships I have with those I am working with. What I have learned is that always the relationship needs to come first and then the project or the work is secondary.

In the world today, most organisations put the project/work first and the employee second. If you really think about it, this approach is not sustainable. People must always come first.

Know that everyone comes into your business life for a reason. Difficult people are there to help you grow. If you need to deal with a difficult person, ask yourself:

- What are the feelings this person is triggering in me?
- What do I have to believe to feel this way?
- Refer back to Chapter 4 to locate the belief.
- Say "I release and let go of the belief _____ And I thank _____ for giving me another healing opportunity".
- Send love, light and blessings to the person.

The need for boundaries

"Having healthy boundaries" is a term that didn't exist when I was growing up. Healthy boundaries were something I eventually learned later on in life. Setting boundaries means not sacrificing anything that you truly value, for another person. We can lay down a boundary lovingly and kindly. We don't need to be harsh or cruel. Client relationships and employee/contractor relationships may require that we practise having healthy boundaries from time to time, such as:

- Healthy relationship boundaries
- Healthy money boundaries
- Healthy time boundaries
- Healthy goods and services boundaries.

Having healthy relationship boundaries

A professional relationship is not the same as a personal relationship. I have seen many people get themselves into difficult situations because they have blurred the line between customer and friend or employer and employee. As much as you can, keep the boundaries clear.

For example, do not socialise on a personal basis with clients unless it is a social occasion for your business. And do not contact your employees or contractors outside of agreed working hours.

Having healthy money boundaries

Be at peace with what you charge and don't allow others to disempower you when it comes to being paid for your goods and services. There may be times when you intrinsically know that the right thing to do is to offer a discount, but you do this from an empowered place, not from a place where you feel you have no choice.

Having healthy time boundaries

Your time is valuable and so is everybody else's. Stick to time boundaries and if you need to go over an agreed time (whether it is a meeting, a session or a service you are providing), acknowledge this with the other person and come to an agreement as to what to do about it. Whether or not someone needs to pay for the extra time is a decision that needs to be negotiated.

We all have the same 24 hours in a day. Do not rob yourself or anyone else of precious time that could be used more effectively.

Having healthy goods and services boundaries

Be clear on what you are offering and ensure you deliver it. If for any reason a customer or client is not happy with what they have received, be sure to address the matter. If you know that you have delivered what you have promised and the client is expecting something above and beyond what you promised, explain the matter clearly but do NOT go above and beyond what the initial agreement was, as you may be setting yourself up to give too much in the future to a client who is perennially dissatisfied. If you know that what you delivered was substandard, address the matter by offering something more that will satisfy the customer.

Financial worries

There may be times when money doesn't flow in or flow well. Remember one simple truth. Money comes from the Source; your customers and clients are one channel through which money comes to you, but there are MANY channels.

When we start to worry about not having enough money, we put a lot of energy into NOT having enough money. If you fall into this thinking, surrender your worries and fears to the Universe and ask that money (and whatever else you need) will come to you in a divine and perfect way. Then give thanks in advance.

Keeping faith

There were many times during the early days of my business where I struggled to have faith and trust that it would all work out for me. I eventually healed my mistrust by keeping an Evidence Journal. In the journal, I would write down regularly every "win" I had, every miracle I experienced, every positive manifestation. When I found myself falling into pessimism or hopelessness, I would read over my Evidence Journal and feel my vibration shift back into faith and trust. You can download a free Evidence Journal from my website.

Always celebrate your wins

Whether it's a new client, a new sale, a successful marketing campaign or any other manifestation of a successful business, celebrate! A prayer of gratitude and making the time to sit with the joy of success, even if it is for one minute, will raise your vibration, magnify that success and attract further success.

"A champion doesn't become a champion in the ring; He's merely recognised in the ring. His 'becoming' happens during his daily routine."

Joe Louis

Crafting Your Spiritual Business Plan

Exercise 19 - Journaling

Creating a Daily Structure

What is my ideal morning ritual?

If you possibly can, include the following

- Wake up time
- Meditation
- Prayer of intention and surrender
- Gratitude
- Exercise

What are my ideal working hours?

What is my ideal end of day ritual?

If you possibly can, include the following

- Bed time
- A pat on the back to self
- Prayer of gratitude

Sunday or Monday Ritual (prepare for the week)

- Plan for the week ahead by writing your to-do list and diarising anything that is important.
- Contemplate what you would like to achieve or manifest and visualise this for a few minutes, until you are in the feeling place of it.
- Surrender your intention to the Source and give thanks.

Exercise 20 - Prayers

A prayer of intention and surrender

Be still and allow yourself to feel quiet and calm. Say the following prayer to the Universe:

I surrender to You this day (or week).
Thank you that I may achieve all that I plan to achieve
May I lovingly accept all that is not achieved,
Knowing that You always know what is divinely right for me.
May this day/week flow with divine synchronicity,
grace and ease.
Thank You.

A prayer for when business is slow

Be still and allow yourself to feel quiet and calm. Say the following prayer to the Universe:

I surrender to You my worries and fears
Because business is slow.
Please fill me with Your Light.
Fill me with peace, hope and optimism
And the knowledge that this too shall pass.
May I make the most of this quiet time
And use it wisely,
Knowing that all good will come to me
In Divine and perfecting timing.
Thank You.

A prayer for when business is too busy

Be still and allow yourself to feel quiet and calm. Say the following prayer to the Universe:

I surrender to You my stress and worry
Because business has become too busy.
Please fill me with Your Light,
Fill me with Your peace and give me a calm, clear mind.
And guide me to the perfect solution.
Thank You.

A prayer for work relationships

Be still and allow yourself to feel quiet and calm. Say the following prayer to the Universe:

*I surrender to You my relationship with _____
Please fill me with Your light
And cleanse me of all that isn't love.
May today I relate to _____ with respect and kindness
No matter how they choose to relate to me.
May today I lovingly set clear boundaries
And be a power of love.
Thank You.*

A prayer for financial worries

Be still and allow yourself to feel quiet and calm. Say the following prayer to the Universe:

*I surrender to You all my financial worries.
I surrender to You my fear that there isn't enough money now,
And that there won't be enough money in the future.
Please fill me with Your Light
And bring to my awareness
That today I have enough
And tomorrow I shall have enough.
And in the future my cup shall runneth over.
Thank You.*

A prayer for faith

Be still and allow yourself to feel quiet and calm. Say the following prayer to the Universe:

I surrender to You my fear and mistrust.
Please fill me with your Light
And clear in me all that is preventing me
From trusting in You.
I give thanks for all past miracles and manifestations
And give thanks that my faith may be restored.

A prayer of celebration

Be still and allow yourself to feel quiet and calm. Say the following prayer to the Universe:

I surrender to You my joy and gratitude
for this manifestation / miracle / opportunity.
Thank You for showing me that I am a powerful co-creator
And that You are the magic behind it all.

Conclusion

It has given me great pleasure to write this book and share with you the truths that I have learned along the way to True Success.

In the appendices that follow, I have provided:

- 21 Universal Laws in the form of an affirmation that will assist you on your entrepreneurial journey
- Affirmations to counteract old self-limiting beliefs
- A simple meditation practice to bring more presence and awareness into your life.

And I wish you love, peace, prosperity and light.

Appendix 1
Affirmations for the 21 Universal Laws

The Law of Abundance

I have within myself everything required to make my earthly incarnation a paradise.

The Law of Acceptance

I accept everything given to me; I resist nothing.

The Law of Action

When I take action towards what I want, the Universe takes me seriously.

The Law of Attraction

What I think, feel and talk about I draw to me.

The Law of Balance

I aim for balance in all things.

The Law of Belief

What I believe I create.

The Law of Challenges

I accept that I will be sent challenges for my growth and evolution.

The Law of Detachment

Even though I have desires, I detach from all outcomes.

The Law of Divine Compensation

All losses are replenished when I take responsibility and forgive.

The Law of Dharma

I am here to find and actuate my purpose.

The Law of Divine Timing

I surrender to the Universe's timing which is always perfect.

The Law of Forgiveness

Forgiveness frees me and allows me my good.

The Law of Giving and Receiving

I lovingly give and I lovingly receive in equal measure.

The Law of Gratitude

When I am grateful for all that I have now, I draw to me further abundance.

The Law of Healing

The Universe has the power to heal me when I request healing.

The Law of Karma (or Cause and Effect)

I reap what I sow.

The Law of Least Resistance

I take action in an easy, flowing and relaxing way.

The Law of Perpetual Transmutation of Energy

I have all the power within me to change my circumstances.

The Law of Protection

The Universe has the power to protect all that I love when I ask for protection.

The Law of Rhythm

There is a time for all things. Thy way and not My way.

The Law of Surrender

I surrender my hopes, dreams and challenges to the Universe, knowing that it is the Supreme Intelligence.

Appendix 2
Affirmations to Correct Old Self-Limiting Beliefs

Self

I now release the past and I am willing to know that I am good enough

My products and services are good enough

People are in need of my products and services

I now release the past and I am willing to know that I am worthy and deserving.

I am worthy and deserving of being paid well for my services.

I have all the resources within me to start and succeed.

The unknown is the field of infinite possibilities within me.

I have everything it takes to succeed.

I now release the past and I am willing to know that I can.

I can move beyond old limitations.

I can do all that I need to do to reach my full potential.

I now release the past and am willing to know that I am important and equal to anyone else.

I am important and my business is important.

I now release the past and I am willing to know that I am wanted.

I am wanted by my clients.

I am wanted by the Universe.

I now release the past and I am willing to know that people are trustworthy.

I attract trustworthy and honest people into my life.

My business attracts trustworthy and honest people.

It is safe to be true to me and my purpose.

It is divinely right to put myself and my purpose first

When I am true to myself, I am true to all those around me.

I now release all past traumas of failures and mistakes.

I release the shame I feel about the past.

There are no mistakes, only lessons.

I lovingly learn my lessons from the past.

I forgive myself and all those involved.

I move forward with hope and optimism.

I accept that things won't always go My way; they will go Thy way

I release the belief that just because things aren't going My way, I'm a failure.

There is no failure, only feedback.

I'm bound to experience failures on my way to success.

Every failure is a learning experience.

All I do I undertake with love, purpose and optimism.

I am worthy and deserving of success.

I accept there is a price to pay for everything.

I am willing to make sacrifices in the short term so as to reap my rewards in the long term.

I let go of the need to control other people.

I allow other people the chance to shine in their own way.

I manage, but I now no longer control.

I see and appreciate the talents and abilities of all those around me.

I choose to trust others.

I choose to trust in life.

Money

I now release the past and know it is safe to talk about money.

I release all shame around talking about money.

Money is simply an energy of exchange

I now release the past and know that there is always enough.

There always has been enough money and there always will be enough money.

I always have enough money for anything that is in my highest good.

Money flows to me effortlessly and easily.

Abundance is my Divine right.

When I receive I also give.

When I give I also receive.

There is a flow of infinite abundance available to all.

I am worthy of doing work that I love.

Money comes to me easily and effortlessly as I let go of old beliefs.

Work and money are exchanged with love.

I am worthy of doing work that I love and making good money.

I allow myself to be wealthy and happy.

Money can create all that is good.

It is virtuous to be abundant.

It is spiritual to be rich.

It is wonderful to be rich.

I can contribute to a better world when I have money.

It is divinely right to focus on purpose and money.

It is safe to talk about money.

I can focus on money and care about people.

I choose to respect and value the money I make.

I choose to use my money wisely.

I now no longer sabotage my wealth.

I stay true to my long term financial goals.

Life

I always have enough time for what is truly important.

Time works with me and not against me.

The Universe gives me the perfect amount of time to achieve my soul mission.

I surrender and let go, trusting in a Greater Intelligence than mine.

I give gratitude for all that I have and all that I shall have.

I choose loving words and actions towards everyone and my good returns to me.

When I lovingly keep the focus on me and my purpose, all good comes to me.

I release all envy and choose to be happy for those who have what I want.

Balance is key to my true success.

I have the courage to move beyond old limitations and to grow.

In presence and awareness. I respond mindfully.

I am a loving presence always.

Appendix 3
A Simple Meditation Practice

Sit in a comfortable position with your back straight, either supported or unsupported, depending on what is comfortable. Some people prefer to sit on the floor cross-legged or in lotus position, while others would prefer a chair, particularly if their hips are stiff.

Close your eyes and begin to feel the inside of your body, starting with the top of your head and working your way down to your feet. Become aware of the spaciousness inside your body, and notice where you are holding any tension or pain. Pay attention to the feeling. Feeling the body is a powerful way of disconnecting from the ego mind.

Now allow yourself to become aware of the outside sounds. Listen to them for a minute without judgment.

Begin to focus on your breath – feeling the sensations of the in-breath and the out-breath for a few minutes.

Your busy ego mind may be continually creating thoughts and feelings, agitation or physical discomfort. At times it may pull you into a fantasy or scenario in your memory, or start making plans for the future. Simply override these thoughts, feelings and fantasies by returning your attention to either the outside sounds or your breath. Do not try to push thoughts or feelings away. Allow them to be there while focusing your attention back on your breath or the outside sounds. Over and over again, you will be pulled into a thought. Whenever you become aware of this, re-focus on your breath or the outside sounds.

Meet whatever comes up with neutrality and allow the space for it to be there. Observe it and let it go.

Surrender to the present moment. – over and over again for 20 minutes.

About the Author

Nicole is a trained Forensic Energy Healer, Transpersonal Counsellor and Life Path Guide who is based in Sydney, Australia. Nicole works with people all over the world, facilitating personal transformation.

She has written four books, A Shift to Bliss, 5 Steps to Finding Love, Soul Magic and Soulful & Successful Business.

Nicole offers free meditations on the app Insight Timer and her online courses are available from her website.

www.ingramcontent.com/pod-product-compliance
Lightning Source LLC
Chambersburg PA
CBHW032038290426
44110CB00012B/855